The Retirement
MIRAGE

TIME TO
THINK
DIFFERENTLY

NANCY J. HITE

THE STRATEGIC WEALTH ADVISOR®

thestrategicwealthadvisor.com

The Retirement Mirage: Time to Think Differently

RAA# 19839297

For more information, please contact:
The Strategic Wealth Advisor
1200 North Federal Highway, Suite 200 Boca Raton, FL 33432
nhite@thestrategicwealthadvisor.com

CPSIA Code: PRV0620A
Library of Congress Control Number: 2020908398
Paperback ISBN: 978-1-7348766-3-5
E-book – Kindle ISBN: 978-1-7348766-1-1
E-book – EPUB ISBN: 978-1-7348766-2-8

DISCLOSURES

TABLE OF CONTENTS

INTRODUCTION

The retirement mirage goes something like this:

So, where do you want to go when you retire? Montenegro? Malta? Costa del Sol? Mars, Venus?

And what do you want to do when you get there and have no more earthly work to do? Fish, hunt, jog, surf, explore? Tennis in Tahiti? Sunbathe in Belize, sipping your sixth margarita? Rocket to the moon in an Elon Musk capsule? Boldly, adventurously ride off into the sunset on your thunderously high-powered jet ski? Go hiking, kayaking, or climbing to the summit of Mount Everest for a selfie with your significant other? Why, you could party all night long on the Punta del Este coastline, then when surf's up in Uruguay, go rapturously off on your surfboard.

Welcome to The Retirement Dream Factory! Attend our complimentary lunch or dinner. Learn about the hidden fees inside your mutual fund or 401(k) accounts. See how our investments can provide all you need to blissfully retire, do whatever you want. Ah, nothing to do but enjoy, experience, explore. You've earned the next thirty-five years off after all that hard work. You've worked like a hummingbird—you're now a free eagle with wings spread wide.

But you know something? If you believe in that retirement mirage, in my opinion, you're dreaming! Or you could be waking from a horrible dream. You're in the Financial Retirement FAIRYTALE Factory.

Well, this book is your wake-up call to smell the coffee and see retirement for what it truly is for most of us in the modern era, a mirage. At best, a subterfuge. A beacon to nowhere. A tempting turnpike to a place that, for many of us, may not exist anymore.

RETIREMENT! is a word from a bygone era, as is the plug-in telephone.

Let's blow the whistle on this outdated concept! Let's concentrate on ways to help us SURVIVE—and THRIVE—in a world where, for many people, retirement is no longer an option.

We need to tell the truth. We need to get REAL. No false hopes. You are most likely going to need to keep earning money for many years rather than spending your remaining years relaxing on the beach, drinking from tall glasses with little hats. The world has changed, yet so many books and articles and get-rich-quick schemes are based on that outdated retirement paradigm. I feel those books need to be placed in the history section.

What's happened? Many things. Demographics, for one. There are now more older people being supported through Social Security and fewer young people available to pay in than ever before—and the trend is accelerating. The drug epidemic is killing thousands of young people each year. Lifespans are increasing. Business is changing. AI (artificial intelligence) is taking over. Still, businesses and Social Security and society are hung up on an outdated concept that's a figment of our imagination. This is what *The Retirement Mirage* is all about. This book will help you think differently, as the world today is different than it used to be. Consider this your wake-up call to adapt.

We do not have a chapter on what to do when it's raining financially. Those of us who understand unpredictable weather patterns (financial as well as atmospheric) have umbrellas in the back seat/trunk ready to open. The arrival of Covid-19 in our environment has brought this idea to the forefront for all of us.

People who think they can medically take care of themselves by searching Google for advice to financially prepare for future income needs will realize that a professional is very helpful to achieve desired medical and financial results.

Markets are not consistent, history tells us. Of course, today's public schools do not teach American history starting with 1776, nor do public schools teach financial literacy like they used to. This book includes a chapter on parents teaching their kids financial concepts. Spend it now, Spend it later or Spend it never® is my motto. Our VALUES determine how we spend or don't spend our money.

Bear markets are defined as periods when the stock market declines by 20% or more from the highest point to its subsequent lowest point, predicated on loss of confidence in the financial system. From 1900–2014, there were 32 bear markets. Statistically, they occur about once every 3.5 years and last an average of 367 days.[1]

In the 1970s, the market dropped 48% over 19 months; in the 1930s, it dropped 86% over 39 months. The most recent U.S. bear market occurred in 2007–2009, when the stock market dropped 57% over 17 months. Another notable bear market is Japan's "Lost Two Decades," from 1998 to present, when market values declined 80%.[2]

Despite the occurrence of bear markets, markets have typically been up more than down throughout history. From 1950 through 2018, for example, the S&P 500 was up 53.7% of days and down 46.3% of days, and the number of up days exceeded the number of down days in every decade.

WHAT IS FINANCIAL WELLNESS?

The downturn in the market of 2008–2009 was an internal financial issue involving banks and mortgage initiations. The downturn in the market in 2020 was caused by a severe virus from China that spread

---

1 WSJ, March 2020, James Mackintosh
2 The Standard & Poor's 500 (S&P 500) is an unmanaged group of securities considered to be representative of the stock market in general. It is a market-value weighted index with each stock's weight in the index proportionate to its market value. Bloomberg, "A Brief History of S&P 500 Bear-Market Rallies and What Follows," Sam Potter and Eddie van der Walt, March 2020.

throughout the globe rather than due to a lack of confidence in the financial markets. Covid-19 became the accelerant to the market decline. It was the fastest 30% decline in stock market history. As a result, the drop in the stock market did not fit the definition of a "bear market." It took the S&P only 22 trading days to fall from its record high on February 19, 2020 making it the fastest drop of this magnitude in history according to data from the Bank of America Securities. The illness, named Covid-19, became a pandemic and caused death as well as market volatility throughout the world due to the uncertainty of its duration.

What is financial wellness? Very simply, financial wellness, like physical wellness, is a focus that can alleviate stress from a person who needs guidance sorting out their financial situation, whatever it may be—a benefit that will make happier, healthier, and more productive citizens.

Be ready for the changes in your life, finances, and mindset. Instead of focusing on retirement (the goal), focus on the process (planning for your income needs in the future). Modern medicine will keep us alive until our late nineties. Your financial plan should extend to age 100. The quality of life will, in most cases, depend on your choices along the way. We need to rethink our careers. We need to continue producing income until our late eighties, so we don't run out of money before we run out of time.

Many people today won't have enough money to create the income stream needed to maintain their current lifestyle unless they win the lottery! According to Brian Levitt, chief investment strategist at Oppenheimer Funds, the average American family wastes 16% of their income on unnecessary expenses such as lottery tickets and unused gym memberships—all of which should be eliminated. Levitt says, "This is not about depriving yourself of experiences and opportunities to go places and enjoy life. It's about knowing what you value most—if you value X, Y, and Z, then you can't be wasting your money on A, B, and C."

So . . . WAKE UP, AMERICA, FROM THAT MIRAGE CALLED RETIREMENT! YOU MAY BE DREAMING! We need a paradigm shift away from that tired old concept, that blissful oasis your parents and grandparents dreamt about—and that you may still imagine in your dreams. For many, retirement is a nightmare, beating us up, causing us pain and suffering.

As the Strategic Wealth Advisor®, I studied and focused on financial stability in people's lives for more than twenty-five years in financial services. And here's what I know about the changes we have made in that time to help alleviate the financial issues tens of millions will face: sadly, there has been far less progress than it appears.

In my professional assessment, despite some rosy projections and advances in products, the financial stress of retirement continues to be too painful, too damaging, too expensive, and too ineffective. The same three recommendations—save more in your personal accounts, contribute to your IRA or 401(k), spend less each year— have prevailed for over a half-century. Most people over the age of thirty-five continue to receive these same financial suggestions their parents received 50 years ago. We need to commit to anticipating, finding, and establishing habits to enhance financial stability throughout our lives.

This book is designed to provide you with guidance and suggest ideas for you to investigate. I'll provide you with the good, the bad, and the ugly of what lies ahead for many of us. So many, alas, haven't even a clue.

Like those in the health field, Certified Financial Planners (CFP®) have learned that earlier detection not only prolongs lives, it helps many live happily for years to come. What's missing from today's discussions about retirement is the admission that current strategies have not been adequate for many; we need to take a 180-degree turn. We now invest a lot of effort into finding minimal answers—why not apply the same rigor and focus to finding a solution for the future?

This book is filled with information and inspiration to help you have a better relationship with your money—so you can have more of it and do more with it.

It is different from other books about money in several ways. First, it doesn't just talk about what you physically do with your finances. It explores what you value and the way you think about money. Those two things can profoundly impact how much money you have and what you do with it—perhaps the most important thing I've learned over the years as the Strategic Wealth Advisor®. I have a client who values owning the Nike Vapor Fly sneaker (which sells for $250.00), even though he is not running any races. I personally drive a ten-year-old car that I purchased from a dealer after it was returned from a 3-year lease. Each person's values have a direct relationship to their spending habits. I share with each that there are only three things you can do with money: Spend it Now, Spend it Later, or Spend it Never®.

Second, this book is designed to be easy to understand and applicable to all readers of any education level or socioeconomic status. If you have been thinking seriously about ways to control and manage your money, saving, providing for your family, and creating long-term future income, this book has valuable information. I encourage young people to read this book to help prepare themselves for the financial road ahead. Unfortunately, the U.S. education system does not currently believe financial literacy is important, so it is not taught in grade school or high school. As a result, most people don't have the tools they need to build solid financial foundations for their futures. This book is designed to help you bridge that gap.

Third, this book is built on the newer modern realities that many financial planning guides try to ignore. The world has changed (and gotten much more complicated). Many books (as well as advertisements) that deal with money matters are based on an old paradigm that no longer exists—RETIREMENT.

Fourth, this book isn't just bland facts and figures, financial tools, or products. Its focus is to educate you on ideas designed to provide a stronger and more satisfying financial and emotional future. My book suggests a process to enable you to achieve financial well-being. Its goal is to give you confidence so you are able to create that future. I know that exploring the details of your financial life can feel frightening and embarrassing. Or you might believe your situation is so unusual that no one could possibly understand, much less give you useful advice. I'll help you see that's not true, and I'm not here to judge. This book is filled with relatable stories of real people from all walks of life who have faced real financial issues, but created the changes they desired—for themselves and their families. I am here to nudge you into action. Will you stumble along the way? Of course, we all do, but you will have the confidence in yourself to keep trying, one small step at a time.

Life can be tough: bad childhoods, poor parenting, lousy jobs, and economic problems conspire to trip us up. Like many others, you might have been dealt some bad hands by fate. The news media can make us believe there's nothing that can be done about our problems. But that's not true. If you're in debt, this book may help you get out. If you want to save, or protect yourself against financial disasters, this book can show you how. If you want to leave your current career and follow your dreams, this book could be a road map. No matter where you are in life, no matter what conditions you're facing, if you're still breathing, you can take control, turn it around, and create the life you want. Start with one small step. If you want to buy a $100 item, start by saving $5 per week. The saving habit is activated by this easy step. Repeat saving of $5.00 every week reinforces the process which will carry over to other financial areas. It's a small (atomic) step now to building your personal financial success.

Imagine what your life would be like if you didn't have to worry about financial obligations. Imagine what it would be like not to just have enough, but *more* than enough—even after paying all your expenses. As you know, life is not just about the money—imagine having more free time to do the things you enjoy with the people you love. Close your eyes and let yourself dream. If you can dream it, this book can help you make it a reality.

By the time you're finished reading this book, my hope is you will have a good understanding of the role of a financial coach and how one can help you on the path to more confident financial decisions and planning for your future. I might not be able to work with you one-on-one as your financial coach (yours may be a family member, a mentor, or another professional advisor), but I am going to show you, step by step, ways to work, plan, save, and invest with the goal of big results. I'm going to be something of a cross between a life coach and a financial coach—because the two are inseparable. My only goal is to help you achieve your desired life—not just reaching your financial goals. How you think about money is just as important as what you do with it—because how you think about money helps you *decide* what you do with it. As Helen Keller said, "Nothing can be done without hope and confidence." Optimism is the faith that leads to achievement, and this book will provide you with that optimism.

The Retirement
MIRAGE

Chapter 1

THE CREDIT TRAP

*A*t fourteen years old, Barbara received her first credit card allowing her to be authorized to charge on her mom's account. Her mom felt the $500 limit would give Barbara some spending money while teaching her how to control her finances. Instead, since her mother paid the monthly credit card bills, Barbara learned credit meant easy money. She just presented the card, and money appeared. What could be easier?

Ten years went by. Barbara got a well-paying job as an architect, which enabled her to get even more high-limit cards. She bought a car new, direct from a dealer (on credit, of course), and filled her apartment with nice furniture. She wore the newest fashions and ate at the best restaurants. Barbara continued along, accumulating debt, until this scenario unfolded at the bank...

"Sorry," the guy behind the thick glass said, "I can't give you another loan."

"What? But . . ."

"It's not me. Computer says no."

"But why?"

"You still haven't paid off the last one."

"But you gave me a payday loan last month."

"Yeah, like I said, you gotta pay that back. Can't help you."

"But how will I eat?"

"Your problem. Can't help you."

"I don't know what I'm going to do," Barbara confessed to her best friend, Tammy, over lunch.

"What do you mean?"

"My debts. They're much too high. I feel like I'm drowning."

"Really? But I thought you had everything under control."

"That's what I thought also, but those stupid student loans . . ."

"But you have more than that?"

"Oh yeah. Five credit cards, a car loan, line of credit. It's bad."

"Any ideas?"

"I'm fresh out."

"I was in debt to my ears a couple years ago," Tammy said.

"You had debt problems?"

"Yeah. Still do. But, now I have hope. I got some help from a friend who was a banker. I will be happy to share some of the things I worked on, and maybe it will help you."

"That would be nice—to have hope again."

"Come on over to my place after work and we'll talk about it."

After work, Barbara showed up at Tammy's apartment. They watched a movie, had some dinner, and then began talking about Barbara's financial situation. Barbara explained what was happening.

"Then I couldn't get a payday loan, and after that, the shoe repairman told me he couldn't fix the heel. Well, I couldn't help myself. I broke down and cried."

"I understand," Tammy said, handing Barbara a tissue. "Your shoes are that old?"

"Can't afford new ones."

"Wow. Well, let's look things over and see what we can do."

"Okay."

"What are your goals?" Tammy asked.

"I just want to get my debt under control—you know, not always be under the gun moneywise."

"Okay, we'll come back to your debt in a minute. Let me ask you this: where do you want to be in three years?"

"Oh, I love my job, but I need to make more money. I'll stay where I am—unless, of course, someone offers me more."

"Are you contributing to your 401(k)?"

Barbara answered, "Yes, because the company matches 3%."

"Well," Barbara said, "I suggest the first thing you may want to do is stop the contributions at this time, take that money, and start to pay down the debt. All right, let's get back to your credit issues. How far are you behind on your payments?"

"Actually, not behind at all. I've kept up to date, but I'm paying as little as I can."

"I understand. From what you told me earlier, you have a car loan, five credit cards, and a line of credit."

"Yes, plus a student loan."

"Oh? How long have you been paying that?"

"Going on ten years now. It doesn't seem to be getting paid off very fast."

"Yeah, that happens to a lot of people. They expect to get a great job right out of college, but often that doesn't happen, so they fall behind on the payments."

Barbara and Tammy discussed each credit card and all her other debt. After that, they moved on to other expenses.

"What do you spend your money on each month?"

"Rent, food, gas, bills, and other stuff."

"What is that?"

"What do you mean?"

"Let's explore the 'other stuff' expenditures. We talked about your income and expenses, and it seems to me you should have plenty of money to spare each month. But you said money is always tight, so what else are you doing with it?"

"I eat out a lot."

"Okay. How much?"

"Every day for lunch. It's too much work to make something to bring with me to work."

"And?"

"I go out every Friday night with my friends for drinks and fun."

"Food?"

"Well, yes."

"Okay. Any habits like smoking, drinking, gambling, drugs?"

"No drugs. I do smoke one pack a day and do some social drinking. No gambling, not even a lottery ticket."

"Let's look at those. Let's see what you spend each month on drinking, smoking, and eating out."

Tammy and Barbara spent a few minutes working out the expenditures.

"Looks like you're spending almost $200 a month on smoking, another $250 on drinking, and almost $500 on eating out. That's a lot of money."

"Hmmm. No wonder money is so tight, and I never seem to have any left over."

"Okay, it's getting late, so let's call it a night. Here's some homework. Get a small notebook that you can carry in your pocket. For the next two weeks, list everything you buy. Don't make any judgments, and don't change any of your spending habits. Just list what you spend. We'll go over it in two weeks. Later, we'll go into things deeper, but let's keep it simple for now."

"Oh sure, I can do that. I feel kinda guilty, dumping all my problems on you."

"Don't worry about it. That's what friends are for. See you in two weeks."

Barbara was right on time two weeks later.

"So, what did you learn?" Tammy asked.

"I spent a lot of money each week."

"Did you get an idea where it goes?"

"Sure. What do we do now?"

"Let's look over what you spend and see what we can do to prioritize. But before we go on, how much do you have in your savings?"

"Savings?"

"That's what I thought. You don't have any savings?"

"I've never saved any money. Why would I do that?"

"What do you do when you have an emergency?"

"Put it on a card."

"For the next two weeks, every time you want to purchase something, take thirty seconds and ask yourself, 'Do I need it, or do I want it?' Now, we will start working on your awareness of where you spend money and on making some decisions each time you think you are about to purchase an item. Continue to keep the list you started in the last two weeks, except this time place a large 'N' next to those items you needed when you purchased them and a 'W' next to those items you purchased that you wanted at that moment."

"I see."

"You need to build up some savings, because you must stop using your credit cards for everything. When you have a problem, such as a broken shoe or whatever, you've got to have enough in savings to pay for it."

"I barely have enough money as it is. How can I save any?"

"My recommendation is that your goal should be to save 20% of each gross paycheck. I know, I know. Most people can't do 20% at first, at least not until they make some adjustments in their spending. But you can save 1% to 2% to begin with and work up to it slowly."

"What kind of changes?"

"There's a lot you can do, but it's best to do one or two things at a time. Pick something you can confront, and let's start there."

"I have no idea where to start. I'm getting confused," said Barbara.

"How about eating out less?" suggested Tammy.

"But I like to eat out, and I hate to cook!"

"How about starting with lunch? Just start making your own lunch, bringing it to work, and putting it in the refrigerator in the office. That might give you more than $100 extra each month. You don't have to cook everything. You can purchase cooked chicken, turkey, tuna salad, or whatever at the market along with cooked veggies, or make a sandwich."

"Really? That doesn't sound too difficult. But I hate making lunch every day."

"Make a lunch plan for three days a week. It won't be easy the first week, but by week two, you will most likely have fun going to the local deli or supermarket and selecting your lunch items. You could check the frozen food case for meals that can be warmed in the microwave at work."

"Ugh."

"I know. There's a social aspect of being with people and eating together. You could bring your lunch and join the group without ordering anything except tea or coffee. It's a good way to start changing your money habits, so it makes for a great place to start."

"What do I do with that money?"

"Put some in savings and start paying down your debt more quickly. See this card?" Tammy pointed to a line on Barbara's list. "You're paying 23.5% interest. That's by far your worst rate. Pay that card off first."

Over the next few months, Barbara confronted her expenses a little at a time. She brought her lunch to work four days a week, didn't run out to buy the newest clothes and accessories, went to the movies once a month instead of twice a week, and even cut down on her smoking and drinking.

"It still seems like magic," she told Tammy. "I have some money at the end of the month! But I didn't get a raise or a new job. It's just there. I'm even saving a bit."

"The money was always there. You just weren't putting it in places that would have a positive effect on your financial life."

"Now I have more to spend, which seems weird, and I'm paying down those credit cards. We are going to celebrate when I pay the first credit card off, okay?"

"Yep. You're well on the way. You've done well, so just keep up what you're doing, pay down those debts, and we'll work on the next steps later."

THE NEW TOY TRAP

In this modern age, you're constantly bombarded by advertising. Even during the drive to work, you're inundated with commercial messages. They've become so prevalent that you may not even be conscious of them, but you can be sure you are soaking up every word. Advertising is everywhere, and it is designed to drive everyone to spend money.

There's nothing particularly wrong with spending money as long as you are still meeting your other financial goals. However, modern ads are designed to work at an unconscious level, being seen over and over and over again to drill in the concept that you must buy a particular brand of sneakers or sunglasses to be cool. It seems as if there's always something that we are being told we *want*, something we must have to make our lives complete. It might be a brand-new car, a video game, a new movie that must be seen on the night it comes out, or that new smartphone that was just released yesterday.

Advertising and marketing have convinced the general public of the necessity of purchasing the newest models of something we already have far more often than necessary. This phenomenon is especially prevalent with automobiles, smartphones, video game consoles, and computers.

The habit of purchasing a new car every few years wastes a lot of money for no good purpose. Unless your automobile is a lemon taking up your time and money, it makes sense to keep a car for at least five to seven years, depending on the amount of driving you do each year. Just remember to keep up the maintenance schedule and get an extended warranty, which will cover most items that are not considered "normal wear and tear," such as tires.

When it is time to replace your car, one way to save money and still get the model you want is to buy a vehicle coming off a three-year lease. Most likely you can get the model you want with low mileage, buy an extended warranty, reduce your personal debt, and still get the car at a significant savings over a new one. This can save you as much as 25% to 30%.

Corporate America has convinced the public that smartphones are also both essential and disposable. It's quite common for many individuals to purchase a new smartphone every year or two. Sure, the newer models might have a few updated, interesting features, but isn't that money better spent towards a vacation or some other form of entertainment? Recently, people waited in line for hours in San Francisco to purchase the new iPhone XS—all for a battery that lasts thirty minutes longer than the previous model. It completely sold out on day one.

When you are tempted to update your smartphone to the latest model, think about waiting two or three cycles. You'll save several hundred dollars right off the top. You can save even more if you don't purchase the newest model, but rather just upgrade to last year's model, which will most likely satisfy your needs just as well as the newest model. Extended warranties will usually offer another twelve months to two years of protection against malfunction and failure on top of the time covered by the original warranty. This will provide some peace of mind.

Because smartphones have taken over much of our time, some people are rebelling and looking to purchase simpler flip phones. Flip phones usually sell for $25 to $200 and are making a comeback because they are compact with taller foldable screens and good sound quality. The iPhone X1, meanwhile, is $999 in 2019. Flip phones call and text; they do not feature the advanced apps that supposedly simplify our lives, but in many instances create too many distractions and produce stress. Many who use flip phones indicate they have become sharper and more organized.

Sometimes, just by waiting a few weeks or months to make a purchase of a new model or version of a video game, smartphone, or computer, you can save hundreds or even thousands of dollars. This is because new products are typically sold at a higher, premium rate as soon as they are released by a company. After the initial rush is over, those prices are often dropped dramatically in order to continue sales. By using good judgment and common sense, you can understand that you don't need to have the newest and "best" model of something as soon as it comes out.

The idea here is to change your viewpoint about what is fun or entertaining in your life. There will always be new, shiny, heavily advertised products to purchase. By ignoring or resisting these offerings, you can give yourself more money to save, invest, donate, or spend on that safari you've been thinking about for years. Sometimes people lose track of their long-term goals as they live their lives day to day. Buying things and living life now can seem to override long-term planning, which is one reason why some people never achieve their goals.

THE CREDIT TRAP

Credit cards make it seem so easy to purchase a new television, a cell phone, Christmas presents, movies and books, and anything else you might desire because it will be paid for at some nebulous future date. Unfortunately, once someone begins down the road of buying on credit, it's very difficult to stop. It's just too easy to use those credit cards and make the minimum payments each month. Credit card companies keep sending you additional cards when they know you will make only the minimum payment. The debt just piles higher, and the stress just gets more painful.

Parents are now providing teens with access to their own credit cards. As a result, buying on credit becomes a habit that is developed early in life. Helping to develop this habit is the fact that the teen's charges are paid by the parents. Credit cards with high credit limits are relatively easy to get, and they reinforce the habit of spending money now, adding to an electronic balance that is out of sight and out of mind.

Using credit cards is similar to stuffing your pockets with your favorite dessert—say, chocolate chip cookies or brownies—and not eating any veggies or protein. Yes, you overcome your hunger, but you are setting yourself up for health issues. You can pay for dinner, even at fast food restaurants, get a haircut, repair your car, or buy a book on credit. Everyone accepts credit cards as payment, either online on sites such as Amazon or offline in brick-and-mortar stores. Unfortunately, all these little (and sometimes not-so-little) charges add up over time into large balances, significant monthly bills, and huge interest payments. In fact, charging on credit can become an addiction, with the so-called addict needing to charge ever-greater amounts to fulfill their fantasies and wants. Using only credit cards that you do not pay off each month creates financial issues.

Credit cards have their place in your financial life—*if their uses are few and far between.* There are several positive reasons to use a credit card. Credit card companies usually guarantee the account against fraud. This means that if someone steals your credit card or uses your credit card numbers to make purchases you didn't authorize, the companies will usually refund the amount of the charge. It can also be very convenient to pay for everything through the month on a credit card. This creates an itemized list of your expenditures that you can use to analyze your expenses or help prepare your taxes. Fixed expenses charged to a credit card—e.g., monthly rent—do not result in increased spending and allow you to develop a credit rating, which is very important should you decide to get a mortgage or borrow money for a business start-up. The interest rate you pay will be affected by your credit score. If you are using a debit card, you are actually losing money. Many credit cards give you cash back each year for purchases you make with them. This could be an easy way to earn several hundred dollars a year just by using your charge card rather than your debit card. Personally, I am always thrilled when I receive my cash-back check each year. I look at it as "found money."

One of the worst things you can do for your financial health, however, is to use credit cards to fill the gap between your income and your expenses. This will just create a much larger problem in the future. Credit cards frequently charge 18% to 24% for unpaid balances. Paying this interest rate will frequently bankrupt the cardholder. Consider what happens when you charge a new $1,500 laptop computer on a credit card charging 18% interest. According to analysis by Debt.org, you'll be billed a minimum payment of $37 each month. If you pay only the minimum, it'll take you more than 13 years to pay off that purchase and cost more than $3,200. If you are not careful, you can, when all is said and done, wind up paying three to four times the cost of everything you charge. In addition, if you do not pay on time, your FICO credit score will be negatively affected.

So-called payday loans are among the easiest but also the worst forms of credit you can get. If you pay such a loan when due (usually within a week or two—they are called "payday" because you are expected to pay the loan off with the next paycheck), borrowing $100 will cost $115 (the original $100 plus a $15 fee). However, if you roll the loan over, you could pay another $15, and if you do it again, another $15. Thus, to borrow that $100 for six weeks, you wind up paying $45—PLUS an annual percentage rate of over 300%.

Payday loans range in size from $100 to $1,000, depending on state legal maximums. The average loan term is about two weeks. Loans typically cost 400% annual interest (APR) or more. The finance charge ranges from $15 to $30 to borrow $100. By comparison, APRs on credit cards can range from about 12 percent to about 30 percent. Even if you decide to responsibly incorporate the use of credit cards into your financial plan, stay far away from the trap of payday loans!

Certainly, if your debt situation is dire, you can consider consumer credit counseling or bankruptcy. It's wise to look at the options available before the creditors start hounding you day and night, and in advance of your accounts being sent to collections. For-profit companies offer to negotiate with your credit card company and try to get them to agree to a "settlement" to resolve your debt. (Typically, the "settlement" is a lump sum payment that is less than the full amount you owe.) With this arrangement, you pay the debt settlement company a monthly payment. Rather than using these for-profit companies, you are able to negotiate directly with your credit card company. Discuss your options with the credit card company. Credit card companies offer several options to help customers manage debt. Debt reduction, debt extension, and elimination of fees and interest charges are the main options available. Creditors typically prefer to extend debt rather than reduce it. It is certainly worth your time and a phone call. The credit card company might be willing to freeze your current debt balance and work out some sort of structured repayment schedule at a lower interest rate. This way, over a period of several years, you can pay off the balance without worrying about 15%, 20%, or higher interest costs. But it is always a better option to find more income or reduce expenses instead. Bankruptcy and similar solutions are very hard on your credit rating and will make it impossible to get credit. They will even make it difficult to find employment, rent an apartment, or get insurance.

One of the jobs of your financial professionals is to counsel you through the rough times (such as being deeply in debt) in the best way possible for your situation. Quite often, they can point out solutions that you missed because they have training in, experience with, and understanding of the options available.

A major part of your financial planning should be to reduce and eliminate any credit card debt. Plan on paying off your credit cards before you start investing your money. Your FICO (originally Fair, Isaac and Company) score and the new UltraFICO score will show drastic improvement and ease your loan approvals. If you are able to obtain a credit card, spend only as much as you can completely pay off each month.

CREDIT SCORING

The Ultra-FICO score is evidence that FICO's scoring model may have become a dinosaur. Launching in 2019 and still being tested at the time of this writing, UltraFICO is trying to attract the self-employed, millennials, immigrant entrepreneurs, and migrant savers, "and give people who may have suffered financial distress but are recovering"[3] a second chance.

The new Ultra-FICO will allow you to voluntarily add data to be considered when predicting your level of credit risk. Specifically, you can choose to allow Ultra-FICO to view and evaluate your bank transaction data (money market accounts, checking accounts, and savings accounts) alongside your credit report for a chance to

---

3   https://superiortradelines.com/news/ultra-fico-score-and-tradelines-everything-you-need-to-know/

improve your credit score. A "consumer-centric" approach to credit scoring is Ultra-FICO's secret sauce.

UNDERSTANDING YOUR COSTS

Working on the expense side of the equation is a great way to create more financial breathing space. It's amazing how much money is spent unnecessarily over time. For example, fees and charges can creep into bank and credit card accounts if you're not careful. Often, these will be waived after a simple conversation with the bank or credit card company. Eating out less often, purchasing a car off of lease, and keeping your smartphone longer can add a surprising amount of money to your budget.

Before you buy on credit, understand the total cost, which is the principal plus the interest and any fees. Buying things on credit can increase the cost of goods and services by two, three, or even four times, especially if you pay the minimum amounts on your cards.

When credit cards are used, the amount of money spent more than doubles. Cash allows you to see what you have and what you have spent. According to a Forbes study in July 2018, shoppers spent up to 100% more when using their credit cards instead of cash to pay for discretionary items. NerdWallet indicates that McDonald's reports its average ticket is $7 when a credit card is used versus $4.50 for cash.

When you're looking at expenditures, it's usually the "other stuff" that's causing the problem. It could be as innocent as eating out at expensive restaurants too often or a hobby, for example. Addictions can be more complicated, especially because people don't want to talk about them or even admit they have them. These are often the things that must be confronted and resolved in one way or another. You might reduce eating out even if you do not cook, for example, or quit smoking or reduce how often you go to the movies. As long as you have enough income to pay the rent, utilities, and transportation, you have the options to make these kinds of choices. For the time being, you may have to move if your rent is really too high, or use local transportation if owning a car is a luxury, not a necessity.

Most of the time, there are many different expenses and spending habits that need to be addressed. It's best to start with something small. Even just making your own lunch three days a week instead of eating out every day can make a huge difference.

Often money can be reallocated, and expenses can be cut by reviewing your current choices and determining which expenses are truly needed and which are wanted. You might try taking thirty seconds to ask yourself, "Do I *want* this item, or do I *need* it?" If you want it, buy it. It's okay. If you ask yourself this question each time you reach for an item, there will come a time when, after thirty seconds, you decide you really do not need it, and you will not buy it. Again, this is a habit that will take some time to establish, but it will provide you with insight into your values and emotions regarding money.

For example, I use this technique: I made a commitment to not purchase a new piece of clothing unless I gave away two pieces of clothing. I have found it difficult to give away clothing, and as a result, I purchase very little clothing. I thought it would be easy to do, but I found it very difficult. My friends now make fun of me because I never go clothes shopping. I keep recycling from the back of the closet.

Keep a list of your expenditures for two weeks. Just write down everything you purchase, no matter how small or insignificant. This will make it easier to find your patterns of spending so you can make informed decisions about spending adjustments.

Chapter 2
THE THREE THINGS YOU CAN DO WITH MONEY

"We're going to the Renaissance festival!" Yolanda's mother said, smiling.

"The festival! The festival!" Yolanda and her little sister, Kelly, jumped up and down with joy, shrieking so loud their mother put her hands over her ears.

An hour later, Yolanda and Kelly smiled as they held their mother's hands, skipping to the ticket booth. What could be more fun than watching jousts, horse acts, plays, and all the other entertainments? Yolanda could hardly wait to go inside.

Suddenly, Kelly turned around, screamed, and ran to Yolanda for safety. She cried, and her little body shook as a goblin in full makeup danced in front of them. It looked terrifying.

"Goblin!" Kelly pointed, tears running from her eyes.

The goblin stopped dancing and approached Kelly slowly. He bent down, came close, and handed her a lollipop.

"Don't be afraid, little girl," the clown said. "I'm just a friendly goblin. I look scary, but I'm really nice to kids."

Kelly laughed as she accepted the lollipop. The goblin reached into a bag, got some candy, and handed a big lollipop to Yolanda. Both children giggled and laughed. Maybe goblins weren't so bad after all. The goblin grinned at the two children and danced away from them—mission accomplished.

Years later, Yolanda accepted a job as a sales assistant in an office downtown. She didn't have a college degree, so she felt lucky to get hired by anyone. Over time, she received several promotions; eventually, she was the manager of the whole department. She knew how to sell, and the company appreciated her talents. Still, after receiving yet another promotion, Yolanda felt something was off.

"Sure, I'm making a lot of money," Yolanda said to a coworker, "but I'm not happy. Is this all there is to life? Working for somebody else who reaps most of the rewards, just to get a paycheck? It seems kind of . . . empty."

"I know," her coworker replied, "but what can you do?"

When Yolanda got back to her desk, she daydreamed and remembered that day at the festival. Now, that was fun! Laughter is a renewable resource.

A few days later, Yolanda was talking to a friend. "It's time for a change. I'm going crazy in my job. Sure, it pays the bills and lets me save a little bit, but it's not what I want to do. I know I want to do something else, but I'm not sure what. And even if I knew, I have no idea how to get there."

"Is there anyone you can talk to about it?" her friend asked.

"I could talk to my mom, I guess."

"She'd agree with your goal?"

"Yeah. She's always been supportive."

"Good. Try to talk to her. I think you can work it out with her help."

A few days later, Yolanda and her mom were discussing what was going on in her life.

"If you could do anything you wanted," her mother asked, "what would you do? I mean, without worrying about money or the opinions of other people or anything else."

"I'd be an entertainer at local Renaissance festivals all over the country," Yolanda said instantly. "I've always loved festivals and the singers. I love the way they make people happy. I want to do that: make people happy, make them laugh and sing. I remember when we went to the festival as kids—for a few hours, you looked happy, like all the weight was off your shoulders for a short time."

"Well," Yolanda's mom said, "you always did like those festivals. But becoming a roving entertainer? That's interesting. Let's look at your current financial situation and see how we can get you from where you are to where you want to be."

"I brought all my credit card statements and a few pay stubs. I figured you'd need them."

An hour later, after going over everything thoroughly, Yolanda's mom leaned back and said, "It seems you like to spend money."

"Yeah," Yolanda said, a little bit embarrassed. "I enjoy life. I'm a little bit of a party girl."

"Nothing wrong with that. I partied a lot when I was younger."

"You did? My mom was a party girl, too? So, that's where I get it from!"

Her mom blushed. "Yeah, I had some fun. After your dad passed away, I had to make some decisions about my life and straighten myself out. I had to support my little girls, after all. But, let's get back to becoming an entertainer. If you want to achieve your goals, you need to make some choices."

"What do you mean?"

"Well, you know there are three things you can do with money. You can spend it now, which is what you've been doing. You've been buying things, going to parties, entertaining people, and having a good time in life."

"Well, yeah, that's true. Isn't that what everyone does?"

"Sure, a lot of people do spend everything they make now. However, that doesn't help you build a future, plan for your future income needs, or start a new career."

"You said there were three things you can do with money. Tell me about the other two."

"You bet," her mom continued. "The second thing you can do with money is spend it later. Put your money aside for emergencies, and possibly in some investments, into savings, for future income funds."

"I've never been good at any of that."

"Well, that's okay. Most people aren't. With you and me working together, we can fix that."

"What's the third thing?"

"Spend it never. This means giving money to charity, donating it to good causes, or someday leaving it to your children or grandchildren. I see you do donate quite a bit to your church and animal rescue funds. That's a good thing because it helps the community and other people. People who give get a feeling of satisfaction and tend to be better off."

"You mean like karma?"

"Exactly. You get what you give."

"This is all a lot of fun, but how do I become a clown?"

"Well, you have a lot charged on your credit cards, but not so bad that you're drowning in debt. Most of your cards are high interest. I see one that's 28%. So, before you start putting money away, you need to pay off these cards. It doesn't make sense to invest and make 8% when you're paying 28%."

"I guess that means I need to stop partying so hard?"

"Exactly. That doesn't mean you need to stop enjoying life. Just stop doing it on credit, and get those debts paid down."

"All right, I guess that's one step towards my goal."

"Yep," her mom replied. "Once you've done that, you'll find you have a lot more freedom in life and a lot more money to do what you want to do."

"I need to attend entertainer school."

"Entertainer school? They have entertainer schools?"

"Oh yes! You have to learn the accents, how to dress, how to act, what to wear. There's one just a few miles from me. I'd like to apply and attend the school in the evenings."

"What does it cost?"

"The one I want to attend costs $2,000 for the whole curriculum."

"Let's add that to your plan. We'll put part of your money towards paying down your credit card debt and part of it toward saving for clown school."

"I shouldn't put the school on my credit card?"

"Not if you can avoid it. From what I see, you could probably have most of your debt paid off within a year. If we factor in saving up for school, it's more like 18 months. Can you wait that long?"

"Of course; I've waited my whole life so far. Another year and a half won't make much difference."

Eighteen months later, Yolanda began attending clown school in the evenings. She was proud of herself. This was the first time she'd paid for a major investment like this with cash instead of putting it on credit.

Six months after that, Yolanda performed for the first time for a local festival in front of an audience of over a thousand people. She sang, danced, and skipped around several stages, making people laugh. She especially enjoyed giving children lollipops, making funny faces, and giving them homemade toys.

Yolanda was well on the way towards achieving her dreams. She was not making enough as an entertainer to quit her job—at least not yet—but at least she was doing something that brought her (and others) pleasure—something more aligned with her goals for her life.

SPEND IT NOW, SPEND IT LATER, OR SPEND IT NEVER®

Did you know there are only three things you can do with money? You might think that's an oversimplification, but it's true. You can **spend your money now**, you can **spend it later**, or you can **spend it never.**

What does that mean? Spending it now should be pretty obvious. This is when you go to the store to buy groceries, you pay your rent or utilities, you pay bills, or you purchase a gift or something fun from Amazon or eBay. Spending it now is exactly what it sounds like: you use your money to get something right now.

Of course, we all must "spend now" throughout our lives. If we don't (unless somebody else is "spending now" for us), we won't have a place to live, we won't eat, and we won't own anything. The problem with spending money now (beyond what's needed for your normal expenses) is that there is no future in that spending. Sure, the rent gets paid, the bills are up to date, and you've got a few luxuries, but without money in the bank for emergencies and future income needs, you are actually creating problems for yourself down the road.

Unfortunately, many of us were not taught the value of delaying gratification as children. This is a difficult value for parents to instill in children because it requires saying "No." Many parents are focused on being friends with their children while they're young, rather than providing them with the financial skills necessary to be successful adults. This is an important skill parents need to encourage in their children, and yes, it is possible. There are some children as young as three years old who have a greater ability to delay gratification, as the famous Stanford marshmallow test exhibited.[4]

Delaying gratification ("spending later") means saving or investing your money to use at a future time. As an adult, that includes putting away a portion of your paycheck into your Roth IRA, Health Savings Account (HSA), or 401(k) each month, or even just squirreling away a few dollars each month into your savings account for emergencies and dream vacations. As an adult it is important to have a minimum of 6–8 months of living expenses in your savings account for emergencies. The recent Covid-19 virus brought this concept into reality for many.

Giving money to charities, donating to your favorite causes, or leaving money to your children and grandchildren is "spending it never." In this instance, you're giving money (or time) to a good

---

4 The Stanford marshmallow experiment was a series of studies on delayed gratification conducted in the late 1960s and early 1970s by psychologist Walter Mischel. Subjects could choose between instant gratification (eat the marshmallow now!) or earn a bigger reward in the future by demonstrating self-discipline and delaying their gratification. Professor Mischel and his team followed up with the subjects over the course of many decades and noticed a direct correlation between their self-discipline and success.

cause, and your personal reward is usually more fulfilling than purchasing something unnecessary for yourself now.

Yolanda had a good career and made a decent living (even without a college education), but she spent it all on partying and other frivolous things. She was stuck "spending it now," so her finances were too uncomfortably tight to afford her the opportunity to pursue her dreams. Once she reprioritized her finances and decided that her goal was important, she was able to shift into "spending it later" by paying off her debts and saving for school. From there, she was able to fulfill her dream—which just so happened to include a strong element of "spending it never," as she brought joy to a whole new generation of kids!

Through recognizing when your money is being spent—now, later, or never—you can truly start prioritizing your finances to fulfill your dreams and accomplish your goals.

REDEFINING "SUCCESS"

Most people believe that they will be happy once they achieve success in their field, make a lot of money, or become powerful. They believe when you are happy and have "made it," you can afford to be generous.

Actually, that's not the way it works.

One of the biggest misconceptions that we learn from a young age is that we must own things to be happy. We are taught that getting a new car or a bigger home will make our lives complete and make other people like us. The belief that happiness flows from objects and success comes from your relationships (parents, friends, coworkers, and so on), the media, advertising, and modern society in general. Advertisers want you to purchase their products, so they promote the idea that you'll be happier once you've done so. Car commercials, for example, present the idea that a new car will get you promoted, make you popular, and give you happiness. Those who don't have a particular car are doomed to be depressed, unloved, and unpopular. Auto leases are usually for three years to encourage us to trade in and continue the cycle of leasing.

Because many people buy into these beliefs, some of the most important things in life get put on the back burner. We become convinced that we must be successful in order to buy the things that we want, which will lead to happiness. It can be very sad watching someone work most of their lives, spending eighty hours a week at the office, trying so very hard to achieve happiness. They think that by making more money, they will be happy and *successful*, as if happiness were a commodity that could be bought on the stock market.

But what would our lives look like if the pursuit of happiness had nothing to do with material objects? What if giving, showing generosity, and expressing gratitude to others were the actual root of being happy? How would life be different if, instead of trying to purchase the newest and greatest toys, we actually gave to others, helped our community, and donated to organizations that support our values?

Maybe we have it all wrong.

I know that sounds counterintuitive; how can anyone become rich, famous, and powerful by giving? Don't you have to become rich and famous first? How can you hope to donate and give without money?

You may need to redefine "success" in your life.

If you take a good look at most truly successful people, you'll find they achieved their goals by giving.

People who give tend to think of more than themselves. They expand their thoughts and consciousness to encompass their communities, their jobs, their religions, their countries, or even the universe.

They think beyond just this paycheck or what they're going to do Friday night. Instead, because others depend on them, their minds tend to plan ahead so that they won't let anyone down.

When you focus on just your own success, whether financial, professional, or something else, your view of the world tends to be very one-dimensional. Your worldview centers on you. How much can you make an hour? How can you get that raise? How will you spend your weekend?

When you give and feel gratitude towards others, you tend to look at the world in a multidimensional way. You might ask how you can help your church to expand, engage your coworkers, or make your community safer. By giving, you encourage other people to give. By helping others, you give them the power to help. They learn from your example, and thus they give and help others as well.

The most interesting fact about giving and gratitude is that the more you help others, the more you get in return. If you are working only for your own benefit, only you receive the benefits of your work. On the other hand, if you are engaged with the community, your profession, your church, or some other group, then many people want to help you in return. To put it simply, if you have no friends, there's no one to ask for help when you need it. Conversely, if you've been helping people in your community and then you find yourself in need of help, you'd be amazed at how many others will jump to your aid.

The path to happiness is paved with gratitude, and happy people are more likely to be successful. Giving to others and helping those in need makes you happy. And when you are happy, you can accomplish more, feel better about yourself, and get more done. In other words, you become more successful, inside and out.

Therefore, I believe it is important that you include giving to charities, supporting your community, and being engaged with others around you in your financial and personal life. It's relatively easy to do. Find something in your area that's important to you. This could be as simple as donating to a cause that rescues feral cats and finds new homes for them or volunteering for a community service or religious events. The charities that you support are completely up to you, and the amounts of *money and time* that you give should come from the heart. Pick causes that resonate with your own beliefs and desires, because it's not just a matter of writing checks to these organizations. It's vital that you participate in the groups that you support. Donate your time. Your time is irreplaceable, whereas money can be replaced. Organizations understand that to be true. Time can be just as or even more valuable than monetary donations.

As you work through this process, think about more than just yourself or your family. Expand your horizons to consider how your actions can help your friends, community, church, other businesses, and even animals (if that's your passion). Not only will you be more satisfied with the result, but you'll create friendships, relationships, and alliances that will be beneficial throughout your life.

The effects that giving will have on your happiness as well as your finances can be immeasurable. You might not always see the benefits, but they are there nonetheless. That seems to be the way that the universe works. You get what you give. If you give nothing, don't be surprised if you get nothing.

Chapter 3

S.M.A.R.T. GOALS

"*G*od, I hate this job," Glenn thought for the hundredth time that day. Life seemed empty. Stocking the shelves of the local supermarket didn't have much purpose. But Glenn wanted a car, and not just any car—he wanted a Mustang.

The next day, he applied for work at a local auto shop. He'd loved cars since he was a young child, and he'd taken a few automotive classes during evenings while he worked at the supermarket.

"Any experience?" the stern-looking manager asked.

"I know how to fix cars," Glenn answered boldly.

"We'll just see about that," the manager replied. He picked up a box of tools and led Glenn out to the shop floor.

"What now?" Glenn asked.

"Something's wrong with that car. Here's the ticket. Fix it."

Two hours later, Glenn had the car running like a top.

He was offered a job and gave notice at the supermarket. A few days later, he started working as an assistant mechanic. Best of all, his pay increased, and he was doing what he loved.

For the next year, Glenn took more classes in the evenings and practiced his craft every workday on countless cars. He was a very fast worker, which pleased his boss because Glenn was able to get a lot done. However, they had some disagreements on the services sold to clients. The other mechanics frequently recommended and performed unnecessary repairs, and they overcharged for labor. Everyone fought for insurance jobs because they could charge outrageous rates for repairs that were never done. Glenn refused to follow their lead . . . but given the negative reviews he then got from his boss, it seemed honesty was not the best policy.

Nonetheless, Glenn was passionate about working on cars, repairing and tuning them so they ran well. He frequently went above and beyond the call of duty to ensure the best service to his customers. He loved the sounds, smells, and textures of cars and engines, and he could often diagnose a problem within minutes.

One day, Glenn's boss suggested intentionally damaging parts and doing shoddy repairs to get more money from customers. As he listened, Glenn realized he couldn't do this anymore.

I'm tired of getting yelled at, Glenn thought, standing outside the shop. *I'm a great mechanic, and my boss knows it. I don't understand why we can't just provide good service to our customers. Why all these con games?*

A few days later, Glenn talked to a bank manager about taking out a loan for a new business. The application was quickly denied because he had no credit history, no business plan, and no collateral.

The bank would have loved to help him out, they assured him, but they couldn't loan money without a reasonable expectation of being paid back.

Glenn complained to his friend Jack as they stood outside the auto shop. "It's a catch-22. You must have credit to get credit. But how can you get credit when you don't have credit?"

"Yeah, I know. But what're you gonna do about it?"

"I don't know," Glenn replied. "I'd like to open my own shop, but I don't how. I need some money."

"Well, you can do what my dad did," Jack replied. "Go see my dad. He will help you so you can reach your goals. My dad had some difficult times, but he says it was the best decision he ever made—starting his own business."

A few days later, Glenn sat in a comfortably padded chair talking to Jack's father, Fernando.

"What are your goals?" Fernando asked.

"I want to start my own auto repair shop," Glenn said, "but I can't get a loan. The bank manager told me that he couldn't give me one. How can I start my business without any money?"

"Are you sure you don't have any money?" Fernando asked.

"I make about $15 an hour, which is just barely enough to live on."

"What assets do you have?"

"What do you mean?"

"You have a car? Any collectible items? Old toys?"

"Oh, I have my car that I use to get to work, and I recently bought a classic rebuilt Mustang. I also have quite a few fantasy and science fiction figures and comic books that I've collected over the years."

"Why don't you get those appraised and see how much money you can raise?"

"I don't know . . . those things mean a lot to me. I've been collecting them since I was a kid."

"Sometimes you need to choose. How important is your goal?"

"It's my life. That's what I want to do."

"Is all the stuff you own as important as that?"

"Well . . . since you put it that way . . . I guess not."

A couple of weeks later, Glenn came back to Fernando to report his progress. The amount of the appraisal on everything that he owned surprised him. Some of the figurines and comic books were worth quite a bit of money, and the classic Mustang was worth even more.

"How much money do you think you can get?" Fernando asked.

"I've already started selling things, and it'll probably all be gone in a week. Looks like I'm going to get about $50,000."

"Your stuff was worth that much?"

"Yeah. It surprised me, too!"

"So, what's your plan now?"

"I found a garage in a commercial area. It's just one bay, but there's a couple of rooms on top. One will be my front office, and I'll sleep in the other one. That'll save me the money of having to get an apartment, plus any commuting."

"You kept your car?"

"Yeah, the old one. It's just a used car, not worth very much. But it'll get me around, and I'm a repairman, so I can keep it in shape. I'm selling the Mustang."

"Have you worked out a business plan yet?"

"Not yet. That's what I was hoping you and I would work on today. Looks like I'm going to have the money to start my dream, but I'm not sure how to do it."

"Great. Have you heard of SMART goals?"

"Nope," Glenn said.

"SMART is an acronym, and it stands for specific, measurable, achievable, relevant, and time-bound. By using this technique, you can set goals that you'll actually be able to meet."

"Can you give me an example?"

"Sure. Let's start with your idea to start an auto shop. You could set a goal of 'I will finance my auto repair shop within 12 weeks without using any debt. That's specific, 'S'—finance my auto repair shop; measurable, 'M'—$50,000; achievable, 'A'—selling collectibles; relevant, 'R'—life goal; and has a time limit, 'T'—12 weeks."

"Yes, I see how that works," Glenn said, after thinking a moment.

"If you always set your goals using the SMART system, you should have no trouble getting what you want. Now, let's take a shot at your financial roadmap."

Fernando and Glenn worked together for the next couple of hours on the financial roadmap for his new business. By the time they were done, Glenn had a good idea of what he needed to do to create a viable auto repair business with his own bay, tools, and skills.

Within a year, Glenn expanded the business and hired his first employee—one of the other honest mechanics from his previous job. A few months later, he expanded into another bay, so that they could work on two cars at the same time.

Glenn's reputation for quality repairs at reasonable prices started to be known around the community. He was approached by several adjusters who suggested taking payments from insurance companies. He was hesitant at first, due to his earlier experiences, but Fernando thought it was a good idea. Glenn began working with insurance companies, and his reputation for honesty continued to grow.

Accepting payments from insurance companies turned out to be a brilliant move, and he formed good working relationships with all of them. As a result, these companies frequently recommended Glenn's shop for repairs. They trusted his judgment, even if his estimates were higher than they desired.

"Sometimes, once I get into a car," Glenn told Fernando, "I find that there's more damage than I thought at the beginning. Because of my close working relationships with the insurance companies, they know that I don't pad the bills. So, if it's necessary to come back with a higher quote, I don't hesitate—because that's the right thing to do for the customer."

Within two years, Glenn, along with three employees, had to move to a new location with three bays and a larger parking lot. Except for the lease on the location, Glenn paid for everything with cash. He didn't feel comfortable buying things on credit, although he made sure he always had a credit line available for emergencies if needed in the business.

Throughout this time, Fernando continued to mentor him. Glenn hired a payroll company for the biweekly employee paychecks and started a health-care plan for all.

After fifteen years, Glenn's business had expanded. He needed more space. He looked around for a property to purchase. He now had three locations with a total of fifteen bays and plenty of parking. Glenn thought owning a property would provide him with some security for the business. This became his next SMART project.

REMAIN TRUE TO YOURSELF AND FOLLOW YOUR DREAMS

How did a young man in his early twenties go from being an employee making only slightly more than minimum wage to owning his own small auto repair shop? And how did he, just 15 years later, come to own an entire chain of repair shops?

Glenn knew that he didn't want to spend his life working for somebody else for pennies on the dollar. He wasn't going to get ahead playing that game. Instead, he decided to create his own business based on his passion, which was fixing cars.

At the beginning, he had a tough decision to make: What was more important? His custom classic Mustang and other possessions, or fulfilling his dream? It's too easy for people to get tied down to their possessions. Sure, it's fun to own toys, video games, cars, computers, books, movies, and other things. But are objects more important than achieving your goals? By pursuing his dreams and cutting loose the car and toys that he'd bought earlier in his life, Glenn succeeded beyond his dreams.

When he began, Glenn thought he would be happy owning his own business, the single bay, fixing cars all day long. But he found that he enjoyed not just repairing automobiles, but the sense of satisfaction that comes with a job well done and a business that's expanding. He always charged the right price for the work done, never padded his bills, and remained fair to both the customer and the insurance companies.

Another choice that Glenn made was to avoid financing his business on credit. Sometimes it makes sense for a business to take out a loan, but you must always keep in mind that loans come with interest payments and must be paid back. By not using credit, Glenn reduced expenses because there was no interest to be paid back.

SMART GOALS

Glenn achieved everything step-by-step by creating SMART goals— one of the most valuable tools we all need to focus on in the modern era that can help achieve desired results.

George T. Doran first presented the concept of SMART goals in the November 1981 issue of *Management Review*. The paper, titled, "There's a S.M.A.R.T. Way to Write Management's Goals and Objectives," discussed the difficulty and importance of setting objectives. The idea was later adopted by Peter Drucker, then expanded on by Professor Robert S. Rubin.

SMART:

SPECIFIC—Let's take one small but achievable change at a time.

MEASURABLE—Make sure you can measure it.

ATTAINABLE— All-or-nothing thinking isn't good. Expect to make missteps—it's OK.

RELEVANT—to your life. Not your brother's or friend's. *Your* life.

TRACK—Get family and friends involved to keep you accountable.

Setting SMART goals will help because they are not just nebulous "pie in the sky" dreams. Setting goals the SMART way means you can more than likely achieve what you set out to do. When your road map is targeted at your life goals, you have a better chance for success because it's more likely that you'll stick to the plan.

Be gentle with yourself, your road map will be filled with potholes and moguls. Remember, life is like a photograph we need the negatives to develop.

Are you actively planning your finances for your future? Or are the challenges of day-to-day life such that you don't have time to think about anything beyond next week's paycheck or what you're going to get the kids for Christmas?

Before doing anything else, identify your short-, medium-, and long-term goals. This is a simple exercise you can do with your feet up, but it creates context and purpose for a financial roadmap and can keep you from veering off track and squandering your earnings. No matter where you are in life or your age, always know how much is coming in and how much is going out.

As you think about your future and the future of your family, it's important to set goals, both for the short term and for the long term, and then create a road map to pursue those goals. Just remember that all roads have curves, bumps, and unexpected delays. I live in Florida, the Sunshine State, but I have an umbrella in the back seat of the car. I never know when it is going to rain. Be prepared for the unexpected in your journey and allow for the detours. You can think of a goal as a target at which you aim your efforts. These can be things such as buying a new car in the short term or changing careers when you reach a certain age in the longer term.

It's difficult to get anything worthwhile done unless you have goals and a road map. Even an informal goal, such as "I want to buy a car next year or two," can help because then you can map out on paper what you need to do to make that happen. Do you have enough money for the down payment, or do you need to save up? Does it have to be a new car, or could it be a car that has come off a three-year lease with low mileage, which would reduce the cost dramatically? This is a wonderful way to get your desired car at a dramatic savings.

Will it be easy? Probably not, but it will be life-changing and fun if you allow yourself to follow your dreams. We are all three people: the public one, the private one, and the secret one we desire to be (the one we review before we close our eyes and nod off for the night). The secret person is the one that runs the record, "could have, should have, would have . . . if . . ." By following your SMART goals, the secret person will be transformed into reality.

MINI HABITS

One of the most important things you can do for your financial success as an adult is to practice or repeat a worthwhile behavior. It doesn't matter whether your focus is sports, ballet, or playing a musical instrument: you must practice regularly to get good at it and have it become a part of your daily routine. Martha Graham, the late, great dancer and choreographer, defined the word *practice* beautifully: "Practice means to perform, over and over again in the face of all obstacles, some acts of vision, of faith, of desire."

When you look back on your childhood, I'm sure you can remember practicing for your piano lessons, shooting hoops, golf shots, baseball swings, mathematics tables, or spelling. The idea is to do something consistently, getting slightly better each time, to enjoy the benefits. This repeated action is not about perfection, but rather about incorporating a behavior you want to make part of your life, whether it be a financial habit, a physical habit, or a health habit. Repetition is not a panacea or quick fix. Practice means continuing to do something until it becomes a habit and feels comfortable. It becomes uncomfortable not to do it and becomes ingrained in your rituals so that it is second nature to you.

I have developed the habit of going to the gym each morning before going to the office. Some of my friends say I am disciplined; however, I find that skipping a day leads to an uncomfortable and uneasy workday. Again, proof to me that the routine of going to the gym starts the day in a positive key. When people ask me if I work out at the gym, I answer, "Only on the days I eat." I usually get a quizzical look, and I say, "Yes, I eat every day."

If you've tried to establish daily/weekly routines and failed, don't feel bad. Your struggle is a common one—and something you can overcome if you understand the psychology behind daily routines. Check out the book *Level Up Your Day: How to Maximize the 6 Essential Areas of Your Daily Routine* by S.J. Scott and Rebecca Livermore or *Mini Habits: Smaller Habits, Bigger Results* by Stephen Guise. A mini habit is a very small positive behavior that you force yourself to do every day; its "too small to fail" nature makes it weightless, deceptively powerful, and a superior habit-building strategy. You will have no choice but to believe in yourself when you're always moving forward. The barrier to the first step is so low that even depressed or "stuck" people can find early success and begin to reverse their lives right away.

The focus on saving money for use later is part of a journey towards greater financial responsibility, independence, and happiness. Ideally, your parents should have begun the saving habit early by saving 20% of all monetary gifts and your allowance while you were in grade school. I remember with my mother, our allowance ritual included a trip to the bank to deposit 20% of the money into a savings account. I remember holding the savings book, the thrill of seeing my name as the joint owner with my mother, and the pride I felt as the amount of money slowly increased.

The rule was that money could be put into the account, but I was not allowed to take money out. I kept the book on my dresser and looked at it each week. In those days, the money in my account earned interest, so I could see that just keeping the allowance actually increased the amount of money that I had available. (Although today in 2020 interest rates remain and continue very low in light of the pandemic, I believe interest rates will begin to increase as the economic environment recovers. Even so, the safety of the bank account, FDIC insured, provides what is necessary for an emergency fund, a special future purchase, or a vacation.)

My mother turned saving into kind of a game by telling me that when the account reached a certain level, we could take some of the money out to get a special gift. So, each time we made a deposit into my savings account, I could see that I was a step closer to the goal of paying for that special gift.

This ingrained in me the habit of saving for a future time, and the practice remains with me to this day. I make sure that at least 20% of any money that I make is deposited to be available later. Every once in a while, I get careless and tell myself, "I don't need to save with this check. I'll make up for it next time." However, I've done this often enough to realize that I'll never make it up with the next check. When I skip the routine, I feel more stress in my life. Sure, skipping the savings deposit for one check does not amount to a lot of money, but not following the habit creates a bit of discomfort. It's kind of like being too tired to brush my teeth before going to bed. Sure, I could get away with that once in a while, but eventually it will lead to expensive dental bills that would have been easily avoidable.

Many of us weren't so fortunate to have parents who instilled this level of financial responsibility in us as children—so it's our responsibility to develop it for ourselves, using SMART goals and building mini habits designed to make it impossible to fail. It's never too early or too late to begin the habit of saving your money. If you can't save 20%, which is the ideal, start from what you can save from each paycheck or payment that you receive. Use the SMART focus. If that's only 1% to begin with, then by all means open a savings account (if you don't already have one) and deposit 1% of the gross amount—create that mini habit. Set a goal with a date for when you'll increase that to 2% or more. Then work to meet that goal. This is not a race to the finish line, it is a financially rewarding journey.

Let's agree and understand that working 10 hours a day in the modern era assists you in making your desired financial life achievable. Now, if you take the extra two hours a day (20%) you work of the day's pay and start a savings account, you will be establishing a solid financial foundation. Let's say you can deposit 2% of your paycheck today and you do so. I'm sure that felt good, putting a little money into a savings account. Give yourself time to adjust to the 2% decline in current spending and see if you are comfortable with the results. Be honest with yourself. Don't judge the time, just let the comfort level become its own habit. Set a goal that next quarter you'll deposit 4% of your paycheck. Before that date arrives, look at your expenses and see what you can cut to meet your goal. Maybe you don't eat lunch out four times that week, or you don't buy something wanted vs. something needed, or you cut something else from the usual budget. Also, look at your income and see if there are any possibilities for making more money. Perhaps you can sell things on eBay, turn a hobby into a money-making business, or even work one day per week in an area you love and put that money directly into savings. If you love golf, maybe you can work at a golf course with the maintenance crew or in the clubhouse kitchen. Be creative, and don't be afraid to think outside the box.

Chapter 4

FINANCIAL BREATHING ROOM

*J*eff was desperate. Five days until payday and he was broke—no food in the refrigerator or gas in the car. He couldn't even feed the cat.

Earlier that day, everything had been going fine. But he'd been driving to work a little too fast on the freeway, and one of his tires blew out. He'd kept the car under control and somehow managed to get over to the side of the road without crashing, but the tire was destroyed. The replacement cost a little over a $125. He paid with a check that he knew would bounce and felt like passing out from despair. How was he going to get through to the next paycheck?

The next day, Jeff visited his aunt Jane, his mother's sister. The two of them had always gotten along well, and she'd helped him out of a few jams in the past.

"Do you need some water? Are you okay?" Aunt Jane asked after letting Jeff into her home. "Honestly, you look ready to faint."

"No, I'm not doing well. Water would be great," Jeff answered. His eyes darted around the room, checking every corner.

"Here you go," Jane said, handing him a glass.

Sitting down in a big stuffed easy chair, Jeff accepted the glass of water and said, "Thanks. I've been under a lot of stress lately."

"Yeah, I can see that. Tell me what's happening."

"My boss is upset with me."

"Really? Why?"

"I asked him for an advance on my paycheck. It wasn't the first time, and he said I need to grow up and solve my own problems."

"Oh? You've asked for advances before?"

"Yes, a few. Now, he says it's a problem that I'm broke, and he says I need to solve it because it's impacting my work and him. But, how can I? My paycheck is just barely large enough to survive."

"Oh—you don't see that as a problem?"

"Well, I guess," Jeff blurted out. "You know, I used to do a lot of couch surfing."

"Couch surfing?"

"Yeah, when I traveled Europe, I slept on a different couch every night."

"Really?"

"Yep. I was young, had no money. Traveled all over the place—France, Italy, Germany, even Romania. Kinda fun, actually. My parents and friends thought I was nuts." Jeff smiled. "I think of those days as the best time of my life."

"How did you survive?"

"Just lived off the land, going from house to house, trading services. They'd let me stay for the night and feed me. In return, I cleaned house, washed clothes, whatever." Jeff shook his head and returned from his memories. "Anyways, I'm used to living on the edge. But, I'm here because of my cat."

"Your cat? Not your boss? I thought you said your boss—"

"Well, my cat triggered it. Missy brought me a mouse this morning, put it right in front of me. She looked at me with those big eyes, and I could swear she was trying to help me by bringing me something to eat."

"You have no food?"

"Nope. Boss wouldn't loan me any money, so I had nothing to eat. And Missy, well, she seemed to be telling me to get help."

"I see. Are you still a bookkeeper?"

"Yes, I'm still a bookkeeper for the same small company. I make about a thousand a week, but after taxes, rent, car payment, and everything else, there's just enough left for food most of the time. I don't always have enough to get food for the cat . . . but she can hunt mice and seems to like them."

"What do you do if there's an emergency?"

"Beg for money from someone or get an advance."

"That doesn't sound like much fun."

"That's how I've lived for over a decade," Jeff answered.

"Oh, well . . ."

"Can you help me?"

"Um, I'm not going to give you any money, if that's what you are asking. But I will help you."

Jeff looked down and said softly, "I just need a little bit to get by."

"Giving you money won't help you. It just prolongs the problem. But I've always liked you, and I don't want to see you in this condition. I'll tell you what—let's look at your income and your expenses, and then see what we can do together."

"Okay." Jeff didn't look happy. "Where do we begin?"

"At the beginning, of course," Jane replied, smiling.

Jeff visibly relaxed and even smiled slightly. He exhaled and took another drink of water, and color came back into his face. "What you want to know?"

"You listed a few of your expenses, but I don't think that's all of them. What others do you have?"

"Well, there's food, gas for the car, a storage unit, and, you know, other stuff, like I said."

"Other stuff? What other stuff?"

Jeff hesitated, then blurted out, "I—this is embarrassing—I like to go out with my friends . . . you know, go to bars, have some fun."

"Oh, really? Is that where you're spending your extra money?"

"Yes. Once a week I go out, eat out, buy some drinks, stuff like that. I spend whatever is left paying for the storage for my old car."

"Okay. How much do you spend?"

"Oh, for dinner and drinks, probably $50, $200 a month for the auto storage."

"Well, it's important to find out where all your money is going. You can use one of the free budgeting tools that banks and credit cards offer online."

"Oh, that sounds like a great idea," Jeff replied.

"How large are your debts?"

"I'm about $20,000 in debt, and my payments are around $500 a month."

"Does that include the principal or just the interest? What interest rate are you paying on this credit card? You need to know this to determine if you will ever be able to reduce the balance."

"I think it's both," Jeff said, looking down at his feet.

"What did you purchase that put you in this much debt?"

"Oh, lots of things. Just books and movies and miniatures for my collection."

"Does your job provide you with health insurance?"

"Yep, medical and dental."

Jane and Jeff talked together for the next hour until she had a good concept of his income and expenses.

"All right," Jane said, "from what we've discussed, it looks like there's some room for cutting expenses. Since you're so close to the edge, try going out with your friends once a month rather than once a week for the next six months, at least until you get things under control. That will help a bit."

"Okay," Jeff replied.

"And Missy will be happy she doesn't have to share her mice with you." Jane smiled.

"But, you know," Jeff said, interrupting, "I'll just spend whatever money is available."

"How about we play a game? Take any extra money you make and put it into a savings account. That way you can be as broke as you want, but you'll have money saved away."

Jeff brightened. "Yes, I can do that! What else can I do?"

"The first challenge is to get you on an even keel so you have enough to get by day to day. How much stuff do you own? I mean, I see that one of your expenses is a storage unit, and you're paying $100 a month for it. What are you storing?"

"That's my mom's stuff. After she passed away, I put her things in storage."

"I see. Have you ever thought of selling them?"

"Not really. I mean, it's my mom's stuff. It would feel wrong to sell it."

"I think she would want you to be happy. She's not using any of it anymore."

"How would I sell it?"

"I've known quite a few people who have used eBay and made quite a bit of money."

"I don't know . . ."

"Think about it. But remember, you don't have to sell it all. Look through it, keep the things that have value to you, and sell the rest."

"That's a great idea! I'll look in the unit and see what's there."

"Yep. Let me ask you a few more questions. Do you think you could take the bus to work?"

"I guess so."

"Do you have a grocery store near your apartment?"

"Yep. It's just a couple of blocks away."

"Got it. So, one option is to sell your car and use public transportation. That would save you in storage fees plus gas each month, but you'd pay for bus tickets instead."

"Hmm. I don't know if that will work."

"It depends on how much you still owe and the value of the car."

"What else can I do?"

"How about taking on a second job?"

"I'd rather not. I'm trying to make time every day to study so I can pass the exam to get certified, so I can make more money in a better position."

"Do you have a hobby that you can turn into a business?"

"Well, yes I do. I like to paint fantasy miniatures."

"You could sell those on Etsy. That's a site for handmade products."

"Oh, nice! Yeah, I could do that."

"Good. I think that's enough for now. You have some homework to do. Give me a call in a few weeks after you've reviewed a few of these options. We can plan to get together. Okay?"

Jeff and Jane talked again three weeks later.

"So, how did you do?" Jane asked.

"I took your advice. I sold a few things on eBay and made $400, which is now in my brand-new savings account. That sure made me feel better, having a little bit of a buffer in case something bad happens."

"Excellent! Anything else?"

"Yeah. I opened an Etsy account and started selling my miniatures. It's amazing. I sold a dozen so far and made another $200, also in the bank. I considered the car, but I can't sell it for a profit."

"I understand. Maybe you can't sell it for a profit, but we need to compare the cost savings—selling would eliminate the gas, insurance, and maintenance costs. And if one tire blew out, the others are probably going to need replacement also—another $500 versus your taking the bus for the next year or two."

"Oh, I see. I didn't think of that."

"That's okay. The idea is to find options, try them, and see what works for you."

"Thanks. I think Missy is happier as well," Jeff said, smiling. "At least she hasn't left me with any mice lately."

"That's good to hear. Keep up the good work. We've only just begun the process. But you'll find that as we work together and as you implement the strategies we discuss, your finances will smooth out, and you'll be doing much better."

BEFORE YOU CAN DO ANYTHING, YOU HAVE TO GET SOME BREATHING ROOM IN YOUR FINANCES

Wouldn't it be nice not to have every little thing be an instant emergency?

Would you feel better knowing that you don't have to worry about finances *now or later*?

Do you think life would be more stable without all that credit card debt hanging over your head?

Living from paycheck to paycheck has, unfortunately, become the norm for many families and individuals. For these people, every day is a challenge, and all minor unexpected expenses become dire emergencies. Without financial breathing room, no planning for the future is possible. Additionally, expenditures such as rent and utilities tend to increase over time, which tends to shrink the amount of money available.

The place to begin a financial foundation is to ensure you are taking care of the basics. Your income needs to be enough to pay the rent or mortgage, pay the bills, and handle your day-to-day needs. If you are not making enough money to even cover your regular expenses, then that is a problem that you must address before anything else. That's because insufficient income will continually put you in danger. You won't have enough to pay your bills, so creditors will start to hound you. You may have to cut down on food, move to a less expensive home, and reduce your recreational activities.

Addictions can magnify your problem, turning it into a regular nightmare. For example, a gambling habit or weekly drinking with friends can quickly soak up all your money and make it extremely difficult to get by from day-to-day. While this book doesn't address addictive behavior, you may have to confront those problems before you can make progress on your financial picture. Professional counseling is available in many communities today as well as through many employers. It takes strength to ask for help. We all need help in some areas. You will be able to move ahead.

When you look at your finances, examine your income (the money that you receive) and your expenses (the money that you spend). Note that many credit cards list the categories of your expenses, which can be great help to give you an idea of where your money is going.

Your first goal is to have more income than expenses. To put it more simply, money coming in must exceed money going out.

If you find you are spending more money each month than what you are earning in income, you must do one of two things:

- Increase your income.
- Decrease your spending.

Of course, you can (and should) do both.

Look at the income side of the equation:

- Can you make more money in your current job?
- Can you work another job?
- Can you turn a hobby into income?
- Do you have things you rarely use that you can sell?
- Do you have any skills that you can use to make extra money?

Then examine the expense side:

- What luxuries can you cut?
- What bills can be reduced or eliminated altogether?
- Can you use public transportation?
- Do you have any addictions that can be addressed?

Once your income is larger than your necessary expenses, your next goal is to accumulate four to six months of living expenses in an EMERGENCY savings account. This is money for emergencies, not for vacations. Emergencies may be medical and dental expenses, housing repairs, auto repairs, and so on.

We normally think of establishing an emergency fund as being a short-term financial goal. However, an emergency fund provides important long-term benefits, which is why it's a good goal for you to achieve. It's SMART:

- **Specifically**, an emergency fund should cover 6 to 8 months of expenses.

- **Measured**, let's say your monthly expenses are $1,200. Multiplied by 6 months, your emergency fund goal will be $7,200.

- **Achieve** this by saving $200 every month from your paycheck.

- **Relevant**, hopefully never, but that's what would make it an emergency!

- **Track** this easily—by saving $200 every month, you will reach your goal in 36 months.

The emergency fund is not a static amount; the fund will change over time as our expenses increase. Because of high interest rates, credit cards should never be used for emergencies unless there's absolutely no choice. Instead, your goal should be to build up sufficient savings that you can get to immediately to use for emergencies and unexpected expenditures. By keeping at least six months of expenses in your emergency savings account, you ensure that any unexpected expenditures are easily handled.

In fact, you don't even have to think about them. A flat tire requiring a patch costing $100 shouldn't even be a concern—it's a disruption, but not a financial concern. Replacing front brakes for $1,000 should be a simple matter of paying for it out of your savings or even the money in your checking account. An unexpected medical bill not covered by insurance can be quite expensive, but if you have money in your emergency savings, you don't need to worry about it. A health plan with a compatible Health Savings Account (HSA) will alleviate much of this issue. With that much money available to you, even a layoff from your job becomes a lot less financially stressful. Sure, you still have a crisis on your hands because you just lost your job, but you don't have to worry about how you're going to pay the rent this month or put food on the table for you and your family. This removes a big source of stress from your life and makes day-to-day living much easier. It gives you a little breathing room. It's one of the secrets of living a happy life.

It may seem utterly unreachable today to have an emergency fund, but just take one step at a time and be patient and persistent. Allow yourself some leeway if your timing is a little off; just get back on track and continue. We are not running a race; there is no blue ribbon for finishing quickly. We are establishing one lifelong financial goal. However, if you put in the discipline to put a little aside from each paycheck, work to cut your expenses, and increase your income in creative ways, you'll find that saving up that money is within your reach. You need to establish this fund prior to investing in your IRA/401(k) or investment portfolio.

Chapter 5

THE SECOND TIME AROUND

*T*rudy and Joel had recently "retired" from their jobs after thirty years. Trudy had been a school teacher who taught American history to high school students. Joel had been a computer engineer. They'd both enjoyed their careers, and felt a bit lost once they both retired.

Also, they were not used to spending twenty-four hours in each other's company.

Trudy and Joel were very adept at adjusting to, settling into, and arranging their lives around long-standing routines and activities. For a significant part of their lives, they had shaped their existence (and portions of their identities) around work. Each of their careers had particular meaning in their lives—meaningful work imbues life with purpose and importance. Undoing these long-standing patterns was emotionally disorienting. This became a huge loss for each of them and they even began to experience some grief during this transition.

Both Joel and Trudy came to realize that being retired was not a happy experience for them. They missed the camaraderie of their former work lives. They also started to realize that although they had tried to plan financially, they had not taken into account their extended life expectancy; they would most likely need additional financial resources to maintain their lifestyle and pay for unforeseen medical expenses in the future.

During his childhood, Joel had fallen in love with the sound of the saxophone and took music lessons. He'd worked his way through college playing sax on weekends at the local coffee shop. Once he began his computer engineering career, he put aside his saxophone and just played it occasionally for personal enjoyment. Casting around for something to do with all this "free time" after retirement, he searched out the dusty old case in the attic and reconnected with his lost love.

Trudy, on the other hand, while studying American history at college, fell in love with the Constitution of the United States. Whenever she had spare time, she would investigate how the founders of the U.S. decided to include or exclude certain passages in the Constitution. Now finished with her teaching career, she found herself continuing her research on the Constitution.

After a few weeks of practice, Joel decided to investigate local night clubs and check out the current saxophone jazz scene. He found small musical groups playing jazz, but they lacked a saxophone player. He auditioned for several groups and was hired to play on weekends.

Trudy decided to put together all her research into a course on the U.S. Constitution. She was able to bring the course to her local adult education department and began to teach three days a week, making some extra money doing what she loved to do.

In fact, both Trudy and Joel are now doing what they truly love on their second time around, and in addition, they're generating extra income to maintain their desired lifestyle.

LIFE SPANS ARE INCREASING

In 1915, the average life expectancy in the United States was 55.1 years. When Social Security began in 1935, the average life expectancy was 62. Age 65 provided a favorable actuarial outcome and appeared to make the system sustainable. As a result, Security payments starting at age 65 would keep the payments at a minimum. By 2007, life expectancy had risen to 77.91 years, and it is still rising. In fact, life expectancy in the United States has been increasing by about two months per year on average (Hanowell, 2016). Due to the current opioid crisis in the United States, life expectancy tables have shown a decrease in the last three years, as noted by the *Harvard Education News*. This is most likely a short-term trend reversal—hopefully it will die off before too many of our children do.

Longer life spans mean that people will be drawing from government social programs such as Social Security and Medicare for far more time than the system was designed to support. Those plans will come under more and more stress the further we get into the future, and if the trends continue, they may have to be redesigned altogether.

You're going to live longer and hopefully be healthier. Now you have to plan how to be happy and maintain a decent lifestyle during those years after your career . . . and the money and planning have to last far longer than you might think.

Focus on planning for your income needs until age 100. I know you just smiled in disbelief, but this is the twenty-first century. In 2020, the United Nations estimated the number of centenarians to rise to approximately 573,000 worldwide. Only a small percentage of us may live until 100; however, with the advances in medicine, good genes, and our focus on nutrition and leading more healthful lives, many of us will live much longer than we currently anticipate.

Planning for future income requires some basic mathematical calculations. For example, if you can get along with $50,000 now, then in 20 years with 4% inflation, you would need $109,556 to do what $50,000 does today. To get $100,000 income from your investments, you would need $2,000,000 earning 5%. If you could find a CD earning 5%, you would not have to worry about market volatility. You could not touch the principal, or you would not have the $100,000. This does not consider taxes and inflation.

SO, IN REALITY, YOU WOULD NEED $3–$4 MILLION TO PREPARE FOR TAXES AND INFLATION.

The focus in the modern era should not be on dying too young, but living too long and running out of money. How much money will you need after you leave your job at retirement age? That depends on a number of factors. Your financial coach will help get the right answer for you.

RETIREMENT AGE

In my professional assessment, the outdated concept of retiring is obsolete, our society and businesses are structured so that people are expected to retire from their careers at a certain age. Retirement in the past was an arbitrary agreement among American businesses, the US government, and the general population that the value of an employee was at an end at a certain age, usually around 65 years old. I know that sounds harsh, and you probably haven't heard it put that way before, but that's the reality. Of course, in the mid-nineteenth century, life expectancy was less than 50 years old. In the mid-twentieth century, life expectancy was around 72, so 65 seemed as good as any number to stop working. Regular monthly Social Security payments started in 1940 because people were living longer, and many were living in darkness and without food. For the first couple of years of Social Security, 1937–1939, payments were lump sum. The first check was for 17¢ to Ernest Ackerman.

Retirement is often promoted because businesses would like to hire younger employees at lower pay than older employees are receiving. Because of this, it's important that you plan your finances so you can be in control of your future. You also need to continually upgrade your skills and knowledge so you can continue to be a valuable asset to the business you work for. Some companies continue to have a required retirement age. Hopefully this will change in the future.

Of course, everybody gets older, but does that really mean that their value declines? Does that mean they can no longer contribute to a business and to society? Our minds do not stop working when we turn 65, 70, or 75. If anything, our experience makes us more valuable. Many of us in the past agreed with the business idea of leaving work when we were 65; however, we didn't spend a lot of time or effort preparing or planning for retirement. Instead, we believed that Social Security combined with a pension or 401(k) would be enough to live on when we left the workforce. In the current time, people are running out of money before they run out of time.

The age to stop working full time is an arbitrary number, a fiction created for convenience. There is no science to support the idea that suddenly, at age 65, a person needs to leave the workforce.

RETIREMENT 2.1

What do we do when our careers in particular fields are over? Then what?

This should lead us to explore what we really love to do, as opposed to what we just like to do or what we're accustomed to doing. Then we need to come up with how and where we'd LOVE to do whatever it is . . . the second time around.

In the modern era, we have to shift our focus to fund education over longer periods of time and to fund multiple careers. We need to plan for longevity and health care. Retirement needs much more than a financial plan. Many couples try to plan financially for the outdated retirement dream without planning for what it will do to their relationship, to their marriage, as now they'll be spending more time together.

In the old days, education and retirement were one-time activities. Rather than a one-time retirement, in the modern era, I believe it is more realistic that we are likely to have sabbaticals.

The concept of sabbatical has been described in several places in the Bible. For example, there is a commandment to desist from working the fields during the seventh year. Strictly speaking, this means a sabbatical would last one year. A sabbatical has come to mean an extended absence in the career of an individual to fulfill some goal, e.g., writing a book, travel, extensive research, and possibly preparing for a career change.

Notice that the word "love" keeps popping up in Trudy and Joel's story.

In the modern era, most people should be prepared to be earning money sixty hours a week. Instead of chasing the outdated non-realistic retirement goal, think about working two jobs—that's right, not one but *two* jobs. One you like because it pays bills and keeps your head above water, the other because you love it. Live on the first job, and save the money you earn on the second one.

Yes, it's important for each of us to develop a "love" activity which we maintain and continue to engage in all throughout our lives. This will most likely become the twenty hours of additional income-producing activity.

Chapter 6

HANDLING A DISABILITY

On his eighteenth birthday, Jose walked into a military recruiter's office.

"What can I do for you, son?" the recruiter asked.

"I want to be a Marine," Jose answered.

"That's great! Just fill out these forms. You have a high school diploma?"

"Yes, sir," Jose answered, taking the clipboard.

"What made you want to be a Marine?"

"I believe in America and freedom."

"Great! Any other reason?"

"Yeah, I want to succeed."

"Oh?"

"I'll become part of a team, learn to lead, and be better prepared to be an adult. Plus, the government will pay for my education."

(This benefit is actually part of the pay program for military service.)

"You certainly have the right attitude."

"Thanks! My family has very little money. I gotta make it, improve, so I can make something of myself."

"You are so right. As a Marine, you'll be in a much better position to confront life, more able to face the world."

Jose finished the paperwork and handed it over. He passed all the tests and within a short time began his training—almost three months of boot camp. He got through it and came out the other side a Marine.

"I'm headed to the Middle East," he told Randy after reading his orders. They'd gone through boot camp together and been friends since the beginning.

"Oh, that's too bad," Randy said.

"Too bad? Really? No. That's why I joined—to support my country."

"You really believe that?"

"Yes, of course."

Randy shook his head. "You're crazy. But, to each his own."

Jose smiled. "What do your orders say?"

"I'll be right beside you. I'm also headed to the Middle East."

A year later, Jose and Randy sat in the back seat of a heavily armored vehicle in Iraq. Their eyes were glued to the surrounding area and their weapons were ready. Even though they were in friendly territory, they knew the enemy could be anywhere.

"Relax," Randy said, constantly searching for anything abnormal outside.

"Sure. I will as soon as you do," Jose replied, his mouth grim.

"Ha. Yeah, sure."

They were interrupted by a terrible explosion. Everything seemed to be happening in slow motion as it ripped through inch-thick metal plates and threw Jose and Randy around like rag dolls in a dryer. Jose closed his eyes and everything went dark.

A noise startled him, and he awoke to see a doctor peering down at his face.

"You're awake? Good."

"Yes, sir," Jose said.

"How do you feel?"

"Like I got hit by a bomb."

"Not surprising, since you were hit by a bomb. An IED exploded under your vehicle. It ripped a hole in the side and tipped the thing over. You're lucky to be alive."

"Oh, how are—"

"No one died. Lucky."

"Where am I?"

"Hospital in Germany. But the news isn't all good."

"Oh?"

"You were hit the worst. We couldn't save your leg."

"Hmmm," Jose said. "I don't know what to think about that."

"We're outfitting you with a prosthetic, courtesy of Uncle Sam."

"For sure?"

"You'll have to relearn how to walk, but you survived."

Jose spent the next few months getting his new leg fitted, learning how to walk, and struggling to recover.

"I'm depressed," he told his brother, who drove him to physical therapy every day. "I don't know what to do. I have no future."

"Well, bro, I've been looking and found someone you need to talk to, the sister of a friend of mine. Her name is Vanessa."

"You think she'll be able to help?"

"Yah, bro. She's the best. She'll know what to do."

A week later, Jose visited Vanessa.

"Problem is, I don't know what's next. What do I do without a leg?"

"What have you had trouble with?"

"No one wants to hire me. Being a cripple makes them uncomfortable. I can see it in their eyes. I wanted to get into computers—you know, security stuff. But now…"

"Hey! You're a Marine! Snap out of it!"

"What?"

"Marines don't give up just because the going gets tough."

Jose smiled sheepishly. "I guess you're right. But what do I do?"

"Your passion. You said computer security. So, focus on computer security. I've read that's a very lucrative field."

"Help me get from here to there."

"Let's look over your finances, discuss your goals, and come up with the way forward."

They spent the next hour discussing Jose's finances, which weren't in bad shape at all. His medical costs would be covered by the US government for a few more years, so that was something he didn't need to worry about.

After an honorable discharge, Jose intensified his job search. Two months later, he found a job doing general computer work. The pay wasn't great, but it helped cover his expenses and made him feel more useful. He worked during the day and went to computer security classes at the local community college in the evening.

Jose continued searching for employment in the computer security industry. He found plenty of jobs, but once employers found out about his disability, they made excuses about why they couldn't hire him. He knew that was illegal, but nothing could be proved.

Finally, he found a good job as a computer security specialist, received an offer, and began working at his passion.

Jose still occasionally met with Vanessa. She helped him organize his finances and figure out how to spend his money wisely, and she encouraged him to continue pursuing his dreams.

"How's the job going?" Vanessa asked.

"Oh, the work is fine. But it's lonely."

"Why lonely?"

"The disability. People are uncomfortable and avoid me."

"Hmmm. How about starting your own company? You could surround yourself with people who don't discriminate."

"I'd like that. Let's work it out."

Vanessa and Jose came up with a plan, and two years later, he teamed up with two other disabled veterans to start his own computer security company. They pooled their savings to fund the start-up and made a point of hiring other combat veterans with injuries. In fact, one of their selling points was that by hiring them, people were helping disabled veterans who had served their countries.

Within two more years, they'd hired a total of eight employees, all with disabilities. The company was very successful and expanded by leaps and bounds with everyone working together as a team.

HARD THINGS

Even with good planning, unexpected emergencies and disasters can occur. A medical expense can come up at the most inopportune time, or an earthquake, flood, or hurricane can cause havoc. Stress can cause people to become ill or emotional and cause all kinds of other symptoms. These things not only cause extreme stress and unwanted depression, but they can also devastate your finances if you are not properly prepared. By maintaining good financial habits along with a stable income, you will go a long way towards decreasing the stress in your life.

Jose was never the type of person to complain about anything. He took life by the horns, always living with gusto, always laughing at any misfortune. To him, losing a leg was just like turning the page of a book to a new chapter. The government provided him with the prosthetic that enabled him to walk, and he had the brains and motivation to turn things around.

Remember, you can turn things around, too. With the right planning and focus in your life, you can achieve your goals and even overcome crippling disabilities. Sure, you may need to talk to experts for advice or to help you through the rough spots, but when you get right down to it, only you can decide to change your life and act on that decision.

When bad things happen to you in life—and everyone experiences them—learn what you can, take stock of your situation, and figure out how to move forward. A life coach and other professionals can help you with this journey by listening and giving you advice and counseling. G-d gives us all a path, which will always have mountains to climb as well as valleys and sharp, unexpected turns that can easily get in the way and slow down our progress. (I spell "God" as "G-d," the way my Orthodox Jewish grandparents taught me.) Maneuvering around the obstacles makes us stronger and more able to climb the mountains, one step at a time. If we remain focused, we will reach the finish line.

What doesn't work is wallowing in self-pity and denial. That's the road to ruin and failure. If you don't confront your misfortune, come to terms with what happened, and create a new future, then your life will not improve, and your circumstances will not change.

Yes, it can be disconcerting when life rips away things that you felt were unchangeable and that you could depend on. You'll feel disoriented, lost, depressed, and stressed. That's all perfectly natural. Allow yourself to experience these rainy days and know that the sun will shine again.

Steady employment brings in money that you can use to pay your rent (or mortgage), utilities, other bills, and food. Having a job also gives a person a feeling of self-worth, of being part of a team, and of satisfaction from a job well done. A job (or self-employment) gives people a purpose, something to strive for.

As soon as you start to take responsibility for the situation, make a plan and the necessary changes, you'll feel better, and daily life will improve. It may take time, and sometimes it may require strong will and effort, but you can make it happen.

BUSINESS IS CHANGING

For most people, the period after starting a career consists of paying bills and climbing their way up the corporate ladder. For others, their dreams include starting their own business. But some people can't always work at traditional jobs in an office with other workers. After getting hired, many find they are not happy with their career choices or that the positions aren't what they expected, or they may not agree with the culture of the business. Nonetheless, they are still obligated to pay those student loans and other debts, pay rent and bills, and try to build independent lives. Their best hope is that as they are promoted or change jobs, their situation and satisfaction will improve.

THE RETIREMENT MIRAGE

In the middle of the last century, it was quite normal for employees to believe they would work at the same company from the time they left high school or college until they retired. However, that world no longer exists (if it ever really did), and the pace of change in business is increasing at an accelerating rate. Mergers and acquisitions of multibillion-dollar companies have become a regular occurrence, and each one of these results in drastic changes in workplace culture and the makeup of the workforce. Thus, while it might be true that you could depend on working for your company for the rest of your career, will it still be true after a merger?

In the past, most businesses required workers to be in an office or other facility. Employees had to commute to and from work each day, which could be frustrating and time-consuming. This method of employment requires that employers provide working spaces, lunchrooms, and other amenities. Assuming these employees are salaried or part-time workers, the business is responsible for withholding taxes, Social Security, and fees for Medicare and unemployment insurance.

A variety of options now exists for every situation. You don't have to remain in jobs you don't like. You may find that some rules seem arbitrary or that established restrictions don't make sense. Examine the situation, do research, and see if there are solutions that better fit your lifestyle, beliefs, and goals. You might be surprised at what you find when you look. Take the time and energy to investigate rather than playing the victim.

There are many opportunities for jobs. Working at home is a great option that you should examine carefully. You can work out of your house full time or as a second job to supplement your income. Temp agencies are another great place to start. These offer, short-term positions. The agencies don't pay much, but they make the effort of finding you work. Do a good job and they will use you more and more frequently. Sometimes you can even get a more permanent position. Keep your eyes open for creative ways to increase your income. Sometimes, small opportunities can result in major revenue in the long term.

With the advent of fast internet connections and cheap computers, it's become possible for employees to work from home or other locations. By taking advantage of this situation, employers can save money on office space, insurance, desks, and equipment. Employees benefit because they no longer need to make that long commute into work. On the downside, it's more difficult to manage employees who can literally be located all over the country—or even in other countries.

Another trend that's becoming more popular among small businesses is the gig economy. This means that employers hire people as consultants. By doing so, the business is no longer responsible for taxes and other benefits. The consultants are handled essentially as small businesses themselves and must do their own accounting. For consultants, there is the inconsistency of work as well as the loss of corporate benefit programs. These self-employed workers will be responsible to pay their own Social Security, and Medicare fees.

What does this mean to you? These trends give you a much greater choice about where you work, give you additional choices to produce income, and provide options for special needs. With a traditional business model of working out of an office, it can be difficult for two wage earners to raise a family since no one is home to take care of the children. By working for a company that allows you to work remotely, you can take care of the children and still get your job done since you're at home while you work. Working as a consultant gives you even greater flexibility because it means you are running a small business. You could, for example, work your normal job during the day and then work as a consultant over the internet for a company in another state on the weekends.

These trends give you tremendous options for increasing your family income. Not only that, but by working remotely, you are no longer limited to businesses that exist within driving distance. This gives you the opportunity to work for companies all over the country or the world. Thus, you can find positions in companies that are a better fit for your goals and income requirements.

Chapter 7

MILLENNIAL DILEMMA

Shandra's life changed overnight. One day she was living at home with her mother, comfortable and happy. She took the courses that looked interesting to her at the local college and worked as a checker at a supermarket, making just enough money for luxuries. The next day, she got into an argument with her mother—money was tight, and her mother needed help with the bills. Shandra refused, claiming she had no money to give.

"Shandra, you've got it easy."

"Mom! No, I don't! Life is hard. I'm in school . . ."

"I need help. Money is tight, and the insurance just went up. Can you contribute something?"

"I gotta buy books for school."

"I know what you spend your money on—cigarettes, parties, and toys."

"I need those things."

"You need to help. I can't pay for you anymore."

"Mom, you don't understand," Shandra said. That had always worked before.

"Tell you what. I have a friend named Tom who has been working with college students for over fifteen years and has experience with the many opportunities and pitfalls students face in college. Why don't you see if he can help?"

"What? I don't need—"

"Yes, you do. You're an adult, and it's time to get a good job, earn your own money, and move into your own place."

Shandra sighed deeply. "If you say so, Mom."

The next week, Shandra met with Tom, introduced herself, and sat down in a very comfortable leather chair.

"Tell me what you hope to achieve," Tom said.

"I don't know. My mom told me to come here."

"Are you okay?" Tom asked, seeing that Shandra was almost in tears.

"Mom is kicking me out. She doesn't understand what I'm going through. College is so hard."

"Why are you in college?" Tom asked. Increasingly, he had discovered that students were in college without much of a clue as to why they are there; all they knew was that it's what was expected of them after they graduated from high school. Tom believed that the sooner Shandra could get thinking about the "why" of her decision, the sooner he would be able to help her with the "how" in terms of how she would go about her collegiate experience.

Tom added, "From trying to study, to living alone and doing the required chores, to maintaining a social life, to possibly working some sort of a job to help with expenses, students don't have the time to manage and think about their time. Does this sound like you,

Shandra? Sleeping in irregular patterns, doing everything at the last minute."

Shandra nodded.

"This kind of behavior is unsustainable; therefore, you need to at least set a rough timetable and start utilizing your time much more efficiently. You will be surprised at the amount of free time you'll start to have on your hands." Tom looked down at his notepad. "What skills do you have?"

"I'm a hairdresser."

"Really? Do you have a job as a hairdresser?"

"Part-time as a checkout cashier. Mom was paying for everything. No need to work much."

Tom's experience had taught him that most college students came to campus with an air of entitlement. Helping students understand this and the significance of making the shift from entitlement to healthy responsibility—and then assisting them with that transition—was key.

"Why don't you get a job as a hairdresser? It seems like you could make quite a bit of money doing that."

"I guess I could, but I would need to take classes and get a state cosmetology license before I could work."

"Well, you definitely won't get a job if you don't look for one. You could take the courses in the evening and work part-time on weekends, maybe as a hair washer, until you get your license."

"When you put it that way . . ."

"Your homework is to put together a résumé and then go out and find a job. Come back in a month, and we'll go to the next step."

"I have never done a résumé."

Tom handed Shandra a sheet of paper with some guidelines:

(1) Organize your information. That is the toughest part. Start with the basics—your education and any part-time jobs you have had.

(2) Keep it short and concise. Get right to the point and let your past experiences do the talking. The entire résumé should fit on one page.

(3) Highlight all your achievements—even great accomplishments that aren't career related. For example, volunteering shows that you know how to work with others toward common goals.

(4) Words are important, so chose them carefully. Action words tend to captivate the reader—e.g., achieved, managed, generated, established, etc.

(5) Review for misspelled words, grammatical errors, and typos. Remember, the résumé is an example of your work.

A month later, Shandra met with Tom again, and her demeanor had noticeably changed. Her eyes were more focused, she was smiling, and her posture had improved.

"So, tell me what happened," Tom said.

"I found a job! I'm working as an assistant to a hairdresser at that salon in the mall. I started last week. I'm so excited. I plan on enrolling in night school to prepare for the cosmetology exam."

"That's fantastic!"

"Yep, but Mom still wants me to move out, and the job doesn't pay much."

"Let's talk about how to use your money. We need to look at your income, or, in your case, your expected income from your new job. Then we'll look at what you need to spend to survive: rent, utilities, auto expenses and travel to work, cell phone, internet, food, and so forth This is step one. Everything else should go into an emergency fund."

"Why?"

"Emergencies. Otherwise, what will you do when something comes up like a flat tire or a dental bill?"

"Credit cards?"

"Oh no! Credit cards are a trap. They make it seem so easy, but eventually you max them out, and then you're in trouble."

"Wow. I have a lot to learn."

"You're an adult, and you can make your own choices. But my recommendation is to put away part of each paycheck—first, into an emergency fund, and then when you've accumulated enough for six months of living expenses, you can direct that portion of your paycheck into investments or a separate vacation fund."

Shandra settled into her new job as a hairdresser. It gave her enough money for rent and the basics, but left little to spare for anything else. After discussing it with Tom, she applied at a temp agency that would give her experience doing a number of different kinds of jobs.

Within a few months, she was able to move out into a small apartment that she shared with a roommate. She even made enough money to send a few dollars back to her mom now and then, just to help out.

TEACHING CHILDREN FINANCES

Children are a wonderful addition to your life, but they require a great deal of your attention to provide them with your values and the support they need. As a parent, you have only 18 years to have an influence on their lives. In reality, you have about 14 years to provide the basic groundwork and educate them about money and the financial world. (The first two to three years, you are teaching them to walk and talk and toileting skills.) Children start school at age four or five, and from that point on, they are influenced by other children with whom they come in contact as well as their teachers. Providing the proper education for children is vital for their long-term success in life—and it should begin much earlier than Shandra's did.

To help children understand the value they bring to the family, it is helpful to have them become contributing members of daily family life when they are young. Do this by having them start with simple tasks that help the family structure: making their beds, putting their toys away, hanging up their clothes, emptying the trash, setting the table utensils for family meals, involvement in caring for family pets, etc. Praising children as they do a good job is a way to encourage continued participation. Values, faith, as well as good health and financial habits begin at home. Parents are part of the solution.

Start teaching them about budgeting and smart spending early as well. Age four is not too young to start. Before you go food shopping with your kids, make a list of what you are going to purchase. Talk to them about buying items the family likes that may be on sale so they can understand the value of purchasing items at the best price. Many stores put a special color tag on the shelf for sale items. This can become a game for kids to find the tags as you walk down the aisle. As busy adults, we have a tendency to rush through the shopping; however, this could become a wonderful teaching and learning experience for your children. Also discuss not purchasing an item because it is not on sale. If your usual brand of toothpaste is not on sale but another brand is, discuss the idea of trying different products that provide the same benefits. Or trying different cookies rather than the usual brand.

It's never too early for a child to begin earning their own income. Once we start giving our children a small allowance, we should use that opportunity to let them know they can make extra money by doing some additional chores around the house. Put a price tag on different chores. This occurs usually around the ages from five to seven. You can also use lemonade stands, school projects, bake sales, and other events as ways to teach your children about finances and money.

You can start teaching the value of money with three jars on the kitchen counter at home. Simply set up three small jars (I like to recommend jam jars because they are not too big and they will fill up more quickly) labeled *Spend (Now)*, *Save (Spend Later)*, and *Gift (Spend Never)*. Start with nickels, dimes, quarters, and dollars bills (which are more easily divided into separate jars). Each child needs to have his/her own set of three jars. Each time children receive money for a task, or as a birthday or holiday gift, they need to take 20% and put it in the LATER jar, setting aside 20% for future items. You may also want to encourage them to put some money in the NEVER jar for those less fortunate than they are. This is money they will donate to a favorite charity, e.g., homeless shelter or animal rescue. You are setting up the SPEND IT NOW, SPEND IT LATER, SPEND IT NEVER® paradigm—the building blocks of their financial education which can provide the stability they need as they become adults. Children do need a structure, says Rialon Berry, clinical associate professor of child and adolescent psychiatry at NYU Langone Health. "Children thrive on routine, which can help them feel safe, regulated and calm," she says.

Once you start paying children for their extra tasks and they have accumulated some money in the Later Jar, it is time to have them open a savings account in joint name with you. Take them to the physical bank; this is part of their education. I know we can do this all online today, but this is a valuable step in their education as well as a special time for them to be with you. The LATER jar has been guiding them to save a percentage of their earnings. This will start them in the habit of saving money for future needs and wants.

Children can use their savings to buy things they may want in the future (SPEND IT LATER), like a new video game or a new school team jersey. We need to encourage children to spend wisely and at the same time provide them with opportunities to make purchases that may not be in their best interest, which will help them learn how to spend their money. Some older children may be encouraged to save money in order to purchase a share of stock in their favorite companies, e.g. Apple, Google, or McDonald's. The important value you are providing is that we don't spend all the money we have; we save some for later and maybe invest for potential growth.

When you take young children shopping, suggest they bring some of their NOW money from the jar with them, in case they want to purchase something. If they want to spend it all on one item, explain they may not have any money left over for the ice cream cone you are planning to get when you finish shopping—later. If they insist they want the item, let them purchase it. When it is time for ice cream, remind them that they have no money left and will have to wait for the next shopping trip, after they have earned more money. Yes, they will most likely start crying and create an embarrassing scene for you. This is the hard part for you, the parent. But this is an important chapter in their financial education even though it may be temporarily painful for you both. If you pay for the ice cream and give in to their tantrum, the learning lesson will be lost. This is a very important teaching moment. Life is like a photograph; you need the negatives to develop.

By the time they are in high school, children's financial needs have increased, you are providing an allowance that has also increased and they should have been given more responsibility around the home. It is important for high-schoolers not to have access to a credit card or debit card, but rather to use cash. Yes, it is easier for you, the parent, to provide a credit or debit card, but the financial lessons will not be provided. In summary, children need to know you are not an ATM. This is a critical time in their financial education. In most situations, children spend their allowance before the school week is complete.

Part-time jobs are a wonderful way to educate children about responsibility, reliability, and engaging with people outside the family. Even when they have a job, we need to continue having children put 20% of their gross pay in their savings account. The LATER JAR 20% goal is the amount they need to save for future income needs. If we educate our children early, they will develop a lifelong habit that will serve them well. This is also a critical time to reintroduce gifting to a charity. Beyond the money earned for completing tasks well, part-time work enables the young person to learn to be punctual, work as a team member, take direction, and become responsible for their actions. These are lifelong skills that can be extremely valuable in young people's future careers.

When a baby chick is trying to break out of its shell, it struggles but persists. If the chick can't hatch, there is most likely something wrong with the chick, and it won't survive. You actually feel terrible for the chick. You may even be tempted to break the shell—but if you do that, you will actually be hurting the chick even more in the long term, because the heart wrenching struggle is what gives it the strength to survive. Recently, we have all witnessed the anxiety and consequences of parents trying to help their children with applying and getting accepted to colleges of their choice. These parents are robbing their children of adulthood. Helicopter parenting (the practice of hovering anxiously near one's children and monitoring their every activity) is so outdated. Some affluent mothers and fathers in this era are more like snowplows: machines chugging ahead, clearing any obstacles in their child's path to success so they don't have to encounter failure, frustration, or lost opportunities. That's a mistake. Life is like a photograph—you need the negatives in order to develop.

These days, it's not uncommon for young adults to remain living with their parents into their mid-twenties or longer. Sometimes these arrangements work out for the best, but often it becomes burdensome to the parents and frustrating to the children. These arrangements can become a sort of trap. A financial coach can help parents and children alike come to terms with these types of situations and create plans to change them for the better of all concerned.

Sometimes the hardest task is just getting started. Even the idea of getting that first job and moving out of your parents' home can seem to be an insurmountable challenge. Likewise, finding new employment (often because a job has become unsatisfying or stifling) can be difficult to confront. Once they finish college, young people face another rude awakening—landing a job is harder than expected, even in today's expanding economy. The competition for good positions, even entry-level ones, can be fierce, and the job market is exceedingly tight at the best of times.

Often, all older children need is to become employed so they can contribute to the upkeep of the household. As young adults, having to contribute to the family expenses, even when not necessary to the family income, is an important learning experience. Sometimes, it's necessary for these young adults to confront not just getting employment, but making enough money to move out on their own. Change is a necessary part of life, and as you grow older, you'll want to be independent. When you have your own place, you get to live by your own rules, and your relationship with your parents may become even closer.

Many options are available to help with income:

- Find one or even two jobs.
- Change your job to a higher-paying one.
- Convert a hobby into a paying opportunity.
- Sell products on the internet.

There are also options to help with expenses:

- Rent an apartment with one or more roommates.
- Review each bill for ways it can be reduced.
- Stop eating out as often or at all.
- Cut down on purchases you *want* and focus more on those items you *need*.

According to Alicia Munnell, director of the Boston College Center for Retirement Research, in a 2006 interview for *Frontline* on PBS, people between ages 25 and 35 are better educated than their parents and grandparents, but they have less wealth than recent prior generations and "are behind in almost every economic dimension including earnings and debt."

Millennials, those born after 1978 and whose ranks have increased due to the young immigrant population, have a completely new set of challenges. They have often attended college, but their education may be unfocused and not oriented towards any particular career. The environment in higher education (this includes high school) often does not adequately prepare young people for the challenges of life and/or the work environment. Many of our public school systems today allow students to submit their assignments late and still receive credit, retake exams, or even show up late to class without any consequences. This system does not prepare students for the work environment they will be facing. In the real world, if you do not complete the job or if you are late to work, you will be fired. In fact, many millennials are shocked by the difference in expectations between college life and the workplace.

IS COLLEGE RIGHT FOR YOU?

From the mid-twentieth century, people have become increasingly focused on earning that all-important college degree. After all, everyone knows that it is a requirement for a good job and an excellent living.

In reality, this has never been the case. In 1950, only about 6% of the US population had a four-year college degree. (According to the Census Bureau, in 2017, 36% of the US population had a four-year college degree.) Many of us have examples of people in our own families who did not go to college, yet obtained financial security. I am the first person in my family to attend college; my father's family emigrated from Russia, and my dad used his mechanical aptitude to start his own TV business because his mother told him his younger brother was the one who would get the college opportunity. But the myth provided educational institutions with the ability to promote themselves and demand ever-increasing sums.

The mistake that many young people make is to go to college and even a university without a good understanding of their goals for life. Summertime jobs while in high school may be one approach for students to help them evaluate areas of interest and guide them to determine a future career path. We need to cultivate our education system, hobbies, and pastimes with a view to providing added income during our longer-than-expected lifetimes. Exposure to the trades should be part of the curriculum in the early education system and encouraged throughout our schooling years. When I was in grammar school, the girls had cooking class and sewing and the boys had shop and auto repair. Now, chefs, plumbers, painters, hair stylists, construction workers, and auto mechanics are gender neutral in the modern era. However, due to budget constraints and the need to shore up teachers' pensions, grade schools have eliminated gym classes as well as trade school classes, I think to the detriment of our children's future financial success.

Getting an education is admirable as long as the courses are preparing you for your chosen field. In fact, schooling is a very important piece of the puzzle for beginning many careers. A specific degree can help you land some jobs. However, in this era, much of the knowledge gained in four-year universities are not focused on the professional and social skills that form the foundations for great careers. Students have a tendency to take courses that do not provide a strong basis in a specific career, and colleges are not held accountable for providing the required education to obtain employment in a student's chosen profession: the curriculum is focused on outdated ideas rather than modern issues.

Unfortunately, many younger people today start their adult lives burdened with massive debt—student loans—from their frantic efforts to get educations at the best possible schools and as quickly as they can. According to a 2019 report by CNBC.org, only about 41% of first-time full-time students graduate within four years with a bachelor's degree; 59% graduate in six years, and 42% never graduate at all, due to financial issues.

Student loans can be a great way to finance your education—if your schooling is appropriate for your career plans. It is a mistake to take out student loans to get degrees in areas you don't really want to pursue as a career (or those that have low employment possibilities). In the modern era, what may be more appropriate is to work part time at a job related to your career goals and go to school part time. Taking classes that apply to a career is expensive and time-consuming. Earning a degree, landing a job, and settling into a comfortable position is often overwhelming, especially when finances have not been adequately planned. A college degree can be useful but is by no means required to find a good job, get promoted, or find a lifetime career. Experience is more important than education in most instances. Throughout your career, engage in continuous education. There are many opportunities to take classes at your local community college or online. Managers are impressed by employees who strive to better themselves and sometimes will even pay for classes. Find your passion and educate yourself in that area.

The "best" college should fit the individual student academically, socially, *and* financially. People should investigate the availability of grants and scholarships with the aid of a specialist in this area.

FIRE

One of the most interesting facets of the Millennial mindset is that they, in large part, have already recognized that the outdated concept of "retirement" is neither likely nor desirable for them. The younger generation's solution is FIRE: *financial independence, retire early*. There are blogs, books, and conferences for the estimated 450,000-plus followers of FIRE. FIRE is more about flexibility to pursue your dreams and ambitions than early retirement, says Deacon Hayes, author of *You Can Retire Early*. FIRE doesn't mean you have to quit your job, says Tanja Hester, founder of the website OurNextLife. Most adherents to this concept are millennials and younger members of Generation X who have college degrees and above-average incomes. Some say they are saving as much as three-fourths of their income, living in smaller homes, and driving older cars. Interest in thrift is flourishing, which is a good thing. However, early retirement is not realistic for most. YNBG—*you need budget guidelines*—just as *you need nutrition guidelines*—YNNG. Guidelines are less stressful than budgets and diets because the latter have denial in their focus. No one enjoys denial behavior.

The downside of FIRE is that early retirement can be very risky. It is very difficult to forecast the cost of living for decades. Yes, the rules have changed, and many understand that the system their parents and grandparents relied on is coming apart. Some of the major issues are unexpected medical expenses along with extended life. Both create very costly financial issues. As well, some who have tried early retirement have found socializing with people who still have a conventional job awkward.

Some suggest going on a *"starvation financial diet,"* which may not be any more successful for people than adhering to a *"starvation nutritional diet."* A more realistic approach: spend some now, save some to spend later, and plan on spending some never.

Chapter 8

LIVING TOGETHER

$\mathcal{D}$ ebbie looked at the bank teller in horror. "What do you mean?"

"The balance of your checking account is zero, as I said before. There's nothing in it."

"How can that be? I haven't taken anything out."

"Let me look," the teller said, typing some things into the keyboard. "It looks like you took out the entire balance last week."

"No, I didn't. I didn't take anything out."

The teller turned the screen around so Debbie could see. "You can clearly see what happened here on the computer screen."

"I see what the screen says, but I didn't do that."

"You have a joint account, don't you?"

"Yes. I share it with my boyfriend, Jim."

"Could he have taken the money out?"

"I don't think he would've done that without talking to me. Let me call him and ask."

Debbie pulled out her cell phone and dialed Jim's number.

"Jim, did you take any money out of our account?" she asked before he could say anything.

"No, I . . . I didn't take any out."

"We don't have any money in our account. If you didn't take it out, who did?"

"Well . . ."

"What happened?"

"You remember I was in an automobile accident a while ago, right?"

"Yeah," Debbie said. "What's that got to do with anything?"

"You remember that we got sued, right? The judgment went to collections, and I kind of forgot about it."

"You forgot about it? How could you forget about it?"

"Well, I did! Anyway, they garnished our bank account."

"What does that mean?"

"The creditor withdrew the money directly from the bank account to pay off the debt—the judgment in the lawsuit."

"But why did they take money from my account?"

"Ma'am," the bank teller said, "it's a joint account. That means that both of you can take money out at any time."

Debbie hung up the phone and stomped out of the bank.

What will we do? We have no money!

LIVING TOGETHER

In today's world, many adults choose to cohabitate (live together) without getting married. They might be couples of opposite sexes or the same sex, or groups of three or more people who live together to share expenses. This frequently occurs in US cities that have a very high cost of living, e.g., New York or San Francisco. "Co-living," in which tenants lease tiny rooms in larger apartments shared with strangers, is a budding real estate trend, often referred to as an extension of college dorm life. Over the past decade, it has grown into a multibillion-dollar apartment industry. Renters have access to living rooms, kitchens, and other common spaces, and services such as cleaning or dog walking are frequently part of the deal.

When people are married, both partners have certain legal rights; when they cohabitate without the benefit of marriage, those rights are reduced. It's wise to write up a cohabitation contract, or an agreement about living together. This written document establishes the ground rules of any financial, property, and/or other arrangements that are known and agreed upon by both parties. This is especially important for any major purchases and if there are children involved. A cohabitation contract or agreement requires the use of a legal advisor, someone experienced in family law.

When it comes to cohabitation, social norms are changing, but the law has not always kept up. Cohabitation was once widely seen as inappropriate, but a recent report by the U.S. Centers for Disease Control and Prevention found that three in four women in the U.S. lived with a partner outside wedlock before age thirty. Cohabitation is also a frequent choice for those over sixty-five years of age.

Some things to keep in mind when you are living together:

- One strategy is to maintain separate checking accounts, but open a joint account into which you both transfer money to pay joint bills as needed.

- Another is to keep the finances entirely separate, in case the relationship comes to an end. This makes it easy to separate things out.

- Keep good documentation of the contributions of each party towards any major purchases of property.

- Ensure that the title or ownership to any major purchases is clear. If one party is paying for it, that party should be on the title or purchase of sale. If both parties are paying for the purchase, then it should be in the names of both individuals.

- Don't contribute money to the purchase of a major asset that is held only in the name of your partner. In the event of a breakup, you will have no rights to that asset.

- Avoid cosigning if at all possible, because if you should split up, you'll still be liable for those debts.

- If you buy a house as a couple, you can do it as "joint ownership with rights of survivorship," which means if either of you dies, the other inherits the property; or you can buy the house as "tenants-in-common," which means each of you owns half the home. Discuss the options with legal counsel.

- Remember that unmarried partners are not entitled to receive alimony-type support in the absence of a clear written agreement that says otherwise (in most states).

- Partners should remain financially independent so that if they split up, they can both take care of themselves. Alternatively, you can work with your lawyer to set up a legal agreement to define the responsibilities of each partner for financial matters if the relationship ends.

- Remember that if there are children involved, either party could be responsible for child care in the event of a breakup, just as if they were married.

- Don't forget the income tax issues in regard to living together. Discuss the details with your financial or tax advisor.

- Finally, discuss setting up a durable power of attorney and health care proxy with your legal representative. These clearly document each of your wishes in the event that you're unable to make decisions for health or other reasons.

- Be sure to talk everything over with a financial professional and an attorney.

The law, in many situations, will treat cohabitating partners no differently than roommates. In many places, cohabitating partners can change that situation with simple cohabitation agreements. For example, they can agree that certain items are jointly owned or how certain items will be divided if they split up. These agreements can be tricky to get right though, and might not be legally binding at all in some states. It always pays to consult a good lawyer if you have concerns.

Extremely large multinational companies make extraordinary profits by fostering the belief that everything is disposable and must be replaced regularly. We seem to live in a disposable world. Fixing mechanical items is limited to mostly large items such as automobiles. As a result, in the modern era, we also seem to have developed a disposable attitude with our personal relationships. Spouses and friends are easily cast off rather than resolving the disagreements and maintaining relationships. This is especially critical to consider when deciding to live together without the legal protections of marriage. It's best to think through these arrangements at the beginning of a relationship, when you're on good terms, so that there's no question about what happens if the relationship comes to an end. Understanding the terms, the rights, and the responsibilities of the relationship ensures that all parties know the boundaries of their agreement.

Chapter 9

FUNDING EDUCATION

"*Y*ou know, dear," Nell told her husband, "I think it's time we started to think about the college education of our two children."

"Oh . . ." Billy replied hesitantly.

Billy and Nell had been avoiding this topic for several months. They both knew it was time to start thinking about how to fund their children's college education, but they didn't understand how to go about it.

"Lucas is thirteen and Olivia is fifteen. It's going to take a few years to save up the money to send them to college. Wouldn't you agree?"

"How on earth are we going to save up the hundred thousand dollars or so that we will need to send them to university? I don't make that kind of money," Billy replied.

"I think there are options that we should look at. I talked to a college counselor yesterday, and she told me there are different things we can consider."

"Ah. That's where you disappeared to yesterday."

"What did you think? That I was out shopping or something?"

"No, no. I really didn't think much about it, although I did wonder where you were."

"Well, the college counselor told me that we should consider community college for their first two years, so they can complete their liberal arts requirements at a more reasonable cost. There's no need to attend a high-priced, fancy college just to get the basics. Community colleges are less expensive, and there's one just down the road from us. The kids wouldn't even need to worry about getting dorm rooms or anything; they could just stay at home."

"I can see how that would save money. But how does it look on a transcript?"

Nell stared at Billy for a moment, then answered, "It shows that we are smart and we know how to get the optimum value for our money. If the kids apply themselves and get good grades, transferring might be easier than applying as a freshman because they will have demonstrated their interest in continuing their education."

Billy smiled. "I like that. How much does community college cost?"

"I think with books and everything, it's less than $4,000 per child per year."

"How does that compare with an actual college—you know, like the state college?"

"The counselor told me that an in-state public college currently could cost approximately $11,000 per year, including the cost of books and the rental of a dorm room. A private or out-of-state university costs far more. Remember, we will have two kids in college at the same time."

"How can anybody afford that?"

"One way is to get scholarships. The counselor mentioned there are also grants available."

Billy asked, "What about student loans? Can't they help?"

"I've been thinking about those as well. Student loans do pay for college, but they also burden children with tens of thousands or even hundreds of thousands of dollars of debt before they've even gotten a job or started a career. I don't think that's a great way to start out in life, so underwater in debt that they don't even have a hope of getting out of it before their thirties or even forties."

"Yeah, that makes sense. I agree; it's probably not wise to fund college out of student loans or any kind of credit, for that matter."

Nell said, "Well, let's look into what we need to do to send each of our children to two years at a community college, followed by a few years at a state university."

A short time later, Billy and Nell sat down with their two children to talk it over.

"Lucas and Olivia," Nell began, "let's talk about your education."

"Oh, Mom!" Olivia replied. "Do we have to? I have homework to do."

"Yes, we have to. You're both at the age where we should be thinking about and discussing your higher education."

"What do you mean by 'higher education'?" Lucas asked.

"That's a great question, Lucas. We're talking about going to a college or university, or possibly a vocational school."

"What's a vocational school?" Olivia asked.

Billy replied, "That's a school that is career-focused, one that prepares and trains you for a specific occupation or trade—for example, computer programming, aircraft mechanics, air traffic control, commercial piloting, or construction management. These are just some of the well-paying careers available. The school may also offer some liberal arts courses similar to a four-year college."

"College is expensive, and we need to start figuring out how we're going to pay for it," Nell said.

"Isn't that a parental responsibility?" Olivia asked.

"Partially," Billy answered, "but to be truthful, we would have a hard time paying for everything required to send you both to college at the same time for four years . . . at least currently. What we want to do is talk over some of the possibilities, so we can start planning and working in the right direction."

"Should we just get a bunch of student loans?" Olivia asked.

"No, student loans should be the last resort. You would have to pay them back, and it could take decades. Do you really want to send a big chunk of your paycheck to the bank every month?"

"I see what you mean," Lucas said.

"Of course, your mom and I have been putting aside a percentage of my paycheck every month; the time you hit college age, that will pay for a portion of what's needed."

"Lucas and I could work," Olivia volunteered.

"Yes, that's a possibility," said their dad. "When I went to college, I worked a full-time job as a waiter at a local restaurant. You two could do something similar."

"What about scholarships?" Lucas asked.

"Since you're interested in basketball," Nell said, "I think that's a real possibility. If you work on your game and become a good enough player that the coach takes notice, then you might get a scholarship. Olivia, we know your focus is science, and there are scholarships available in that area as well. Or perhaps there are grants available. Both scholarships and grants don't have to be repaid."

"That sounds ideal," Lucas said.

"So, you see," Nell said, "our best strategy is to come up with a combination of things that we can do, so that when college arrives, you both won't need to worry about how to pay for it."

"I like that, Mom," Olivia said. "You're pretty smart. So, Lucas and I should keep our eyes open for jobs and take classes in high school that relate to our areas of interest that may provide scholarships and grant opportunities."

"Exactly," Nell said. "I would like you both to think about college options. Let's review whatever ideas you've come up in a couple of weeks."

A month later, the whole family sat down once again to continue the discussion.

"It looks like we might be able to get you a scholarship," Lucas said to Olivia. "I've been checking all around, and there are several academic performance scholarships and even some scholarships for women you could be qualified for."

"That would be great," Olivia said.

"A caution, though," Nell said. "I've been doing some research, and it's important to understand that scholarship money usually needs to be spent on tuition, certain fees, and required costs. Some scholarships will cover room and board, but those are not qualified education expenses, so that portion might be taxable."

"What if I live on campus?"

"That doesn't matter. Also, any food or other expenses that are not directly educational are not qualified."

Olivia asked, "What does it mean to be not qualified?"

"That means that the money, even though it came from a scholarship, is considered income. Even though you will never see the money, you will have to pay taxes on it. A scholarship is qualified only if it is used for educational expenses, such as tuition and fees, books, courses, supplies required for certain classes, and so on."

"Oh," Olivia said. "What does that mean to me?"

"It means that any money that you use from the scholarship for anything other than educational expenses, you'll have to include when you file your annual tax return, along with money you earned by working a part-time job."

"That shouldn't be too hard."

"I don't think it'll be difficult," Nell said. "It's just something we all have to plan for so that we're prepared."

EDUCATION FUNDING

Educating children is one of the most important responsibilities of parents. A good education can mean the difference between children who grow into adults who stay at home or struggle for most of their lives, and those who transition into adulthood, move out on their own, and do well.

There are many factors to consider when you are planning your children's education. There are also quite a few solutions available, each with their own advantages and disadvantages.

There are several methods that you can use to pay the cost of schooling:

- You can save up the money. Most states have 529 college saving plans. Many parents start saving early in their working career; others, such as Billy and Nell, start saving when their children are high school age. The more you can save, the better it will be when college arrives.

- Family members can work for the money. Many young adults work their own ways through college by having a job in addition to going to school. Sometimes parents work two jobs or both spouses work in order to pay for their children's schooling.

- Tax benefits are available to help with education.

- Scholarships and grants are available as well.

- Loans can be taken out to pay for tuition and other expenses. Some parents will borrow against their home or other equity, others use credit cards, and many young adults get student loans.

- Families can get subsidized educational loans for their children too, not just the children themselves. These are often a part of financial aid packages.

Many choose student loans because they feel pressured to go to the best school as soon as possible. Guidance counselors and loan companies also push hard to get students to accept these loans. Doing so provides guidance counselors with the ability to verify greater success with student placement, resulting in higher personal ratings. After all, there is a lot of money to be made in the student loan business.

There are many options to consider before taking out a loan to pay for college. These should be the last options on your list. Generally, student loans should be avoided if possible. There are other avenues to explore before choosing to put yourself or your children into debt for the rest of their lives.

Grants and scholarships are available for students with disabilities, certain cultural backgrounds, or specific talents. These are excellent ways to fund higher education, and they are not just for those students who are unusually smart or have some athletic talent. Every year, billions of dollars are awarded to people and organizations. The money comes from all different sources and varies as to amount and time of year that the money is given away. Funding programs have eligibility criteria. Grants and scholarships do not have to be paid back, and they are used to cover all or part of the tuition for school.

Most people don't know about the variety of grants and scholarships that exist. Sometimes, it is helpful to locate a scholarship expert or financial advisor whose focus is providing help locating and applying for these funds because if you are like most Americans, you just don't know where to start.

Financial aid based on need is given only to low-income families. If your income is more than $100,000, you will not qualify for this kind of aid.

There are also ways to reduce the expense of college:

- Community colleges or state colleges or universities in your local communities tend to be less expensive than private schools. There are also varying degrees of selectivity for all of them. As a student, you need to be scrupulous about making sure the courses you take are transferrable from the beginning. Many majors in a four-year school require courses that must be taken in the first two years of school, so you must make sure they are available at the community college. As a final consideration, students often have some difficulty fitting in to the social and even academic scene at another school.

- Your young adults can live at home until they are finished with college, thus saving the expense of renting a room near school.

- Many universities and colleges will offer discounts. You should definitely talk with school counselors to find out options in this area. Remember, colleges are businesses, and in general, they are willing to negotiate the cost of attendance even if they won't admit to it openly. State public college and universities are pretty rigid, usually by law, but there may be more room for negotiation available at private institutions.

- Apply at different schools, everything from community colleges all the way up to universities, and negotiate with them for better pricing.

If you or your children do need to take out a loan for them to attend college, federal student loans should be considered first because the interest rate is fixed regardless of the credit history of the student and a cosigner is not needed.

College funding should be planned well in advance of your children reaching college age. Many parents begin planning when their children start high school, but optimally, saving and planning should begin much earlier. This will give you more choices when the time comes to choose schools and consider the options of how to pay for them.

BE SURE TO HAVE FUN IN LIFE

It can be tempting to dwell on the harshness of life and to focus on how difficult it is to earn that income, pay the bills, and raise children. While you're streamlining your finances to make your life more stable, you might believe that you cannot have any fun in life. After all, one of the central themes of good finances is to limit purchases to things that are important and needed rather than buying on the spur of the moment. A lot of this book is about saving money, investing, putting part of your current income aside to fund future income, and purchasing protection for stormy days.

But what about fun? Is there any room in all this to consider having fun? What about vacations? Presents for Christmas or other holidays? Romantic dinners out on the town? What about buying that new video game that looks so enticing or even going to the movies? In other words, everything we've talked about so far seems to be so serious. What about fun?

Focusing on the problems and the negatives will create stress, anxiety, depression, and even cause health issues. It's therefore vital that you add balance to your life and focus on the things that make you and your family happy and help you grow and prosper.

One of the primary advantages of stable finances with savings equaling six months of income needs, a growing future income fund, college planning, and investments is that the stress and pain associated with not having any money in the future fades into the background. You'll no longer be in financial distress all of the time, scrambling to figure out how to get money for the newest emergency, education for your kids, or even something as minor as new tires for your car. This stability alone will do wonders for making you and your loved ones feel happier and more satisfied with their lives.

Of course, it's nice not having to stress about having enough money to do anything at all. But remember, as you work through correcting and planning your finances, be sure to build in a certain amount of fun. Life without a fun break can be stressful. We need to allow ourselves to engage in activities that give the mind and the body a break. Our focus in this book is on alleviating problems we can see and some we cannot see today. We want to have a seat belt on our finances, but that does not mean we will not have unexpected financial situations.

For you to be happy and to provide your family with an atmosphere in which they can be happy, you must take time out of your hectic schedule to stop and smell the roses. Otherwise, you're just working for the sake of working, and the fruits of your labor will be wasted.

Contrary to what advertisers want us to believe, happiness does not require spending vast sums of money. You don't need to buy things to be happy, and a collection of objects stored in your garage is not going to help your mental condition. In fact, the stress associated with having to pay the bills for those things can easily negate any positive benefits.

Happiness consists of time that you spend doing the things in life that bring you and your family joy and make you feel good. A picnic while on a trip to the beach can cost just five dollars for parking and be much more fulfilling than the newest smartphone, watch, or sneakers.

One of the great things about having stable, well-planned finances is knowing that you can go on vacation once in a while without creating excess credit card debt. A vacation may be taking an extra-long weekend, including Friday and Monday, and playing golf or tennis or going skiing. Short breaks like this are energizing. Planning long vacations—two weeks—can often produce stress. You have to finish the office work before you leave, and when you return, the desk is stacked, resulting in added stress. You feel as though you have not been away.

When you're short on money, even buying a night at your favorite burger spot with the family can stretch the budget to the limit. But when your finances are well planned, you have the freedom to go to the places that you've always wanted to visit and experience them to the limit. The important thing to remember is to budget the cost of any luxuries and pay with cash or, if you use credit cards, to be sure to pay off the balances each month. In general, it's a bad idea to pay for things like vacations, groceries, luxury items, and eating out on credit cards unless you pay off the balances monthly.

Chapter 10

ACTIVITIES OF DAILY LIVING

"Sally, going home for the day?" Manuela asked.

"Yeah," Sally answered. "It's been a long day. I want to get home, make some dinner, and curl up with a good book."

"You and your books. You should go out, have some fun."

"Nah. Tonight, I'm going to read a book. For me, that's fun."

"Well, the girls and I are going out. You're welcome to come with. You got a boyfriend yet?"

"No. I still live alone."

"I don't know if I could do that," Manuela answered. "You've lived alone for a long time. What would you do if something went wrong?"

"Never thought about it. I'm doing very well all by myself, thank you very much. I appreciate the thought, Manuela, but I'm going to pass tonight."

"Suit yourself."

Sally went outside and walked to the corner to wait for the bus, just as she did every work night. She had her nose buried in a book while she walked, not really paying attention to where she was going. Suddenly, she tripped over a tree branch that had fallen across the sidewalk. She thrust her arms out, and both hands hit the pavement hard. Her body had enough momentum to keep going, and her face slammed into the concrete.

Sally closed her eyes, then opened them. She thought only a few seconds had passed, but she was no longer outdoors.

"What's that noise?" she whispered.

"It's our siren. You're in an ambulance," a young man's voice said.

As her vision cleared, she saw him looking at her with concern. He shined a light into her eyes, frowned, and then smiled. "Don't worry; you're going to be fine."

Sally nodded, closed her eyes, and drifted back off.

A few days and several surgeries later, Sally felt frustrated.

"Why can't I close my hands?" she asked her doctor.

"Well, as I explained before, when you tripped, your entire body weight landed on your hands and arms. Your right wrist shattered, your left wrist was sprained, and you broke your nose when your face hit the pavement."

"Yeah, I understand that," Sally said. "But it will all heal, right?"

"Your wrists will never be the same again," the doctor said. "It will take several months of physical therapy before you're able to use them at all, and that's after we take out the pins from the one you broke."

"How will I survive if I can't move my hands?"

"You're going to need help," the doctor replied. "You're not married?"

"Nope," Sally replied. "Never found anybody I liked that much."

"Do you have any friends who could help out?"

"I don't know, but I suppose someone will help."

"What about family?"

"Both parents died, and I don't really have any other family."

"I understand. I'll send someone to talk to you about the various options for home care."

"Home care?"

"Yes. A nurse or some other professional will need to come by your home several times a week, if not daily, to help you out until you can perform routine tasks on your own."

"Oh," Sally said, tears flowing down her cheeks. "I see. It was so dumb, tripping on the tree branch like that."

"It's just a bad roll of the dice," the doctor replied.

"What do I do? I've got disability insurance, which will help, but I don't think home care is covered under that or my health insurance policy. I don't want to and certainly can't afford to stay in an assisted living center. If I'm out on disability, will I ever be able to go back to my job?"

"I don't know the answers to those questions," the doctor said. "I'll send the counselor over to talk to you, and perhaps they can help you come up with a solution."

HEALTH CARE IS CHANGING

Health care will change beyond recognition in the next few decades. The entire medical profession is undergoing phenomenal changes with the advent of robotics, nanotechnology (extremely small things such as tiny robots the size of molecules), telemedicine, cloning, and wearable devices. These changes will result in longer lives and healthier bodies.

Today, illnesses and diseases tend to be diagnosed based on symptoms that occur after an infection or disease occurs and spreads, and most insurance plans require a diagnosis prior to agreeing to pay for screening procedures. On the positive side, better screening techniques have reduced death rates for cancer by 25% in the last twenty-five years. However, there is still little focus on prevention and early detection, since that would require more frequent visits to the doctor's office and expensive testing even when there's nothing visibly wrong. Telemedicine may be changing this aspect of medicine also.

This is quickly changing due to wearable medical tracking devices. These can be worn or implanted within the body to monitor a person's physical activity, blood chemistry, heart rhythms, breathing, and just about anything else imaginable. Instead of going to the doctor after you've been ignoring stomach pain for six months, these wearable devices will be able to detect body changes before an ulcer forms, cancer becomes deadly, or an illness attacks the body. As you can imagine, detecting a disease or condition before it becomes serious can dramatically reduce the costs of treatment.

Wearable medical devices and telemedicine are two trends that will make it easier to remain healthy and receive care from health professionals. Trips to the doctor's office for physicals or diagnoses will become much less frequent in the future. If you feel ill, instead of driving to the doctor's office, you will just set up an appointment using your smartphone. During your appointment, you and your doctor will use video chat to talk about your concerns. Common medical tests can be performed with devices that transmit the information to your doctor. We will no longer have to wait ninety minutes in the cold waiting room for a fifteen-minute appointment.

X-ray technicians will be replaced by computers that can read x-rays more precisely than human eyes can. Procedures that were previously unimaginable because they were too complicated or precise to be done by a human surgeon will easily be performed by tiny robots or surgical machines. We have already started to see this in practice.

LIVING HEALTHY

Medicine continues to focus on creating ways for us to reduce health risks and not only lead longer, but better quality lives. Of course, one of the most important things you can do to be healthy (now and in the future) is to take responsibility for your personal health.

The greatest gift you can give yourself is your health. Genes play an important role; however, you have the ability to mitigate some major issues. By eating the proper foods, exercising regularly, minimizing the amount of stress in your life, and living a healthy, drug-free lifestyle, it's likely that you will have a long, high-quality life. We all want to live a long time, as long as we do not have a condition that destroys our quality of life.

The place to start when dealing with health issues is to lead a healthy lifestyle. You will find many people focusing on the lifelong process of leading a healthy lifestyle. One of the many benefits is you will most likely find new friends along the way.

- **Eat healthy foods most of the time.** Fast food restaurants many times provide food high in fat, sugar, and salt. Many government regulations require listing fat, sugar, salt, and more on the menus. However well-intended these regulations may be, most of us have no idea what the optimal amounts are.

If you regularly consume more calories than you burn, you'll gain weight. Although food labels use a 2,000-calorie diet as the benchmark for average calorie consumption, that amount could prompt weight gain in some sedentary people of small stature. For other people, a 2,000-calorie diet provides too few calories and may result in weight loss. Your individual metabolism determines what is right for your needs.

Most of us can eat just about everything and anything we like; however, what we cannot do is eat as much as we desire. I have found switching to a luncheon-size plate versus a dinner-size plate for meals has helped me reduce the amount of food I consume at each meal. Yes, occasionally I go back for seconds, but only occasionally. Overconsumption is the cause of many health issues. The most successful sugar substitutes have all been discovered by accident. Saccharin was invented in Baltimore about 130 years ago by two chemists at Johns Hopkins University who were experimenting with coal-tar derivatives. By 1968, Americans were consuming 17 million pounds of saccharin per year.

Recent observations in a live telecast concerning Covid-19 by Dr. Anthony Fauci, a leading immunologist in the United States, and Dr. Deborah Brix, the State Department AIDS official and renowned HIV/AIDs expert, both mentioned a sensitivity to the Covid-19 virus with high BMI Index.

Although modern medicine has increased our life expectancy, we need to take responsibility for our own healthful lifestyles. The highest proportion of overweight and obese people—13% of the global total—live in the United States, a country which accounts for only 5% of the world's population, according to a first-of-its-kind analysis of trend data from 188 countries. The CDC reports for 2015–2016 indicate the prevalence of obesity was 39.8% and affected about 93.3 million US adults. According to the Department of Health Metric Sciences in 2013, an estimated 160 million Americans are either obese or overweight. Nearly three-quarters of American men and more than 60% of women are obese or overweight. These are also major challenges for America's children—nearly 30% of boys and girls under age twenty are either obese or overweight, up from 19% in 1980.

The Institute for Health Metrics and Evaluation (IHME) is an independent global health research center at the University of Washington. A study by the group in April 2019 found better eating could prevent one in five deaths worldwide. Low amounts of healthy foods, including whole grains and fruits, is more significant than high levels of unhealthy foods. Dietary risks, such as high sodium intake, are an 'equal opportunity killer.' Poor diet is responsible for more deaths globally than tobacco, high blood pressure, or any other health risk, according to Dr. Ashkan Afshin, lead author on the study: "We are what we eat and risks affect people across a range of demographics, including age, gender, and economic status."

Poor diets were responsible for 10.9 million deaths, or 22% of all deaths among adults in 2017, with cardiovascular disease (CVD) as the leading cause, followed by cancers and diabetes. They also resulted in 255 million disability-adjusted life years (DALYs), which equal the sum of years of life lost and years lived with disability. Poor diet represents 16% of all DALYs among adults globally.

These statistics signal medical issues for the entire country and restrict our population from continuing to have financial stability thru added income.

There's a fine line between being too busy and too lazy to do something. (A survey found that 40% of millennials in a survey believed that *cereal was an inconvenient breakfast choice because they had to clean up after eating it.*) But regardless of whether work deadlines or following Selena Gomez, the singer-songwriter, on Instagram is keeping you from going to a store to shop for food and cooking, the demand for ready-to-eat food seems to be growing.

Many of us in the modern era eat on the run. As a result, even vending machines are becoming suppliers of healthy foods. Two start-up companies, Farmer's Edge and H.U.M.A.N., are providing fresh salads and locally sourced organic food to vending machines.

- **Exercise regularly.** The human body is made to move and be exercised, so include a daily regimen of walking, swimming, or some other physical activity you enjoy to keep your body in shape. Exercise also helps reduce stress and may help you sleep soundly at night.

- **Avoid smoking, addictive drugs, and excess alcohol.** The dangers of tobacco smoking are well-known and thoroughly documented. Smoking tobacco significantly increases the risk of getting cancer of the nose, stomach, liver, kidney, or cervix, just to name a few.

  Smoked marijuana and smoked tobacco are, chemically, very similar. Analyses have identified at least 6,000 of the same chemicals in marijuana smoke as are present in tobacco.[5] Research shows that approximately 20% of regular pot smokers (and it takes only three or four joints a day) complain of chronic bronchitis, coughing, and excess mucus.[6] More research is ongoing as marijuana becomes legalized around the country. You can increase your likelihood of avoiding breathing issues by avoiding smoking anything.

Despite the advances in medical science, life expectancy has actually declined in the United States over the last three years due to current opioid use. Avoiding addictive drugs and limiting excessive alcohol consumption will be incredibly beneficial for your health, safety, and finances.

- **Don't text or talk on the phone while driving.** A variety of studies have proven that texting or talking on the phone while driving is more dangerous than drinking and driving. Even though all fifty states have enacted laws that prohibit texting while driving, many of these laws are not enforced by police; many accidents occur due to the distraction, and the number of people dying annually keeps increasing. Nowadays, a lot of people do not have phone conversations; they can deliver their entire thought through a simple text message. The biggest age group affected by this problem is sixteen- to thirty-year-olds.

  Alabama's first conviction of manslaughter while texting and driving resulted in a two-year prison sentence followed by eight years of probation. The texting driver momentarily took his eyes off the road, swerved into oncoming traffic, and collided head-on with a twenty-four-year-old woman's truck. She was thrown from the truck and died of her injuries; she was not wearing a seat belt.

---

5 International Agency for Research on Cancer (IARC)
6 Truth Initiative® non-profit public health organization

Cognitive scientist David Strayer at the University of Utah says driving and talking on the phone, even hands-free, is a dual task problem for the brain.[7] Most people don't appreciate the parts of the brain involved with attention, planning, and language. Talking on the phone uses some of the same brain space that driving does. So, if you're trying to do both, at least one of them is going to suffer.

- **Minimize stress.** There are many ways to do this, including ensuring that your work is aligned with your personal goals and keeping your finances stable. Avoid criminal activities, such as shoplifting, theft, or worse, which can cause extreme stress and lead to a loss of income or freedom.

You can take a variety of other actions to improve your chances of living a long and healthy life, too. By avoiding habits that are known to lead to health problems and by cultivating habits that help your health, you will increase your chances of living a longer, healthier life.

ACCIDENTS HAPPEN

However, accidents happen and health issues do crop up from time to time, no matter how diligent you are about protecting yourself. Even the healthiest people can find themselves in the emergency room for conditions as simple as food poisoning or as complicated as cancer or influenza. You may also have or contract a chronic condition, such as diabetes, that requires constant care.

Sometimes, bad things just happen—the person driving behind you rear-ended your car, or, like Sally, you could simply trip and badly injure yourself. Anything can unexpectedly happen at any time to ruin your plans. It's likely that at some point during your life,

---

7   https://www.youtube.com/watch?v=LoLtyqa5tEg

you or someone you are close to will be injured in an accident or come down with an illness. With good luck, you'll get through it just fine. Sometimes, longer-term care is needed. For your financial health as well as your own medical health, you must be ready for these eventualities.

HEALTH INSURANCE

It's essential now and in the future to be covered by a health insurance policy of one sort or another. These plans often cover routine examinations, provide prescription drugs at reduced or no cost, and help fund medical intervention after an accident or when you have a serious illness. These policies are vital for your financial health, because an illness or accident can be extremely expensive. It's not unknown for a single trip to the hospital to cost tens of thousands of dollars. If that isn't covered by insurance, the amount comes out of your pocket. Talk to your insurance agent about what kind of health insurance policy is best for you and your family.

If you work for a corporation or business, they probably provide health insurance for you and optionally for your family. If not, there are many options available on the open market, but these can be expensive. However, it's important for your peace of mind to maintain health insurance. Subsidies are available for those who earn below a certain threshold, allowing just about anyone to get medical insurance for themselves and their family.

Due to the high cost of health insurance today, many insurance companies are offering indemnity plans. Indemnity health insurance plans allow you to direct your own care and visit almost any doctor or hospital you like. The insurance company then pays a set portion of your total charges. Indemnity plans are also referred to as "fee-for-service" plans. They have become popular due to the lower premiums.

These types of policies often have relatively high deductibles and coinsurance limits. A deductible means that you are responsible for paying for medical expenses up to a certain amount before the medical expenses are covered by insurance. The coinsurance limit means that once the deductible is satisfied, the insurance company will pay a percentage of each bill until a certain threshold is reached, at which point they'll pay 100%. You will be responsible for the amount the insurance company does not cover—your coinsurance amount. Another good reason to have an emergency fund of a minimum of 6 months of living expenses which includes the deductible for your health insurance.

Congress has agreed that all medical policies will be required to accept preexisting medical conditions and thus not decline coverage. Your rates may be increased but you will not be declined coverage.

HSA

One way to reduce the monthly cost of your health insurance policy is to purchase a plan with a compatible Health Savings Account (HSA), then open an HSA with pre-tax money to help pay for deductibles, copayments, and other medical expenditures. (This is not to be confused with a Flexible Spending Account (FSA) which requires you to use the funds annually or lose them.) The money and assets in a Health Savings Account are portable and belong to you. The money in the HSA grows and can be invested to help accumulate money for future medical expenses. Paying for current premiums may not be the most efficient way to use the funds. You should check with your financial coach and review your options, as many employers have these plans available.

HSAs offer three tax benefits:

(1) **Contributions are tax deductible**: Like with a 401(k), you contribute pre-tax dollars to a HSA, which reduces your taxable income for the year.

(2) **Earnings grow tax-free**: You can invest your HSA contributions and the growth of the investments accrues tax-free.

(3) **You can withdraw money tax-free** if it's used for qualified medical expenses. You can find a list of these expenses on the IRS's website (your HSA provider should also be able to provide you with a list).

The expenses covered through your HSA should be primarily to alleviate or prevent a physical or mental defect or illness, including dental and vision. With a letter of medical necessity from a doctor, even expenses like gym memberships or mattresses can be recommended to treat specific medical conditions and would be considered qualified medical expenses and be paid with Health Saving Account (HSA) funds.

Another advantage is that the money deposited into an HSA is not taxed as income when you put it in, or if your employer contributes to it, as with your 401(k), nor when you use it to pay for medical expenses. Friends, family members, or really anyone else can contribute to your HSA by writing a check payable to you. These contributions do count toward your annual contribution to the Health Savings Account. The 2020 HSA limits were $3,550 for an individual or $7,100 for a family. You need to check these limits because they increase each year. My professional assessment having worked with many retirees over the years, is that the future tax savings opportunity for medical expenses provided by an HSA is very valuable.

Unlike Flexible Spending Accounts (FSAs), the money you contribute to an HSA does not expire. If you don't use it during the year you contributed, you can keep rolling it over even if you get a new job.

Each year, the IRS issues health plan guidelines that include the limits you will be required to pay out-of-pocket, as well as the amounts you are allowed to contribute to the HSA. Out-of-pocket limits include deductibles, copayments, and other amounts, but not premiums.

HSA-compatible health options are often positioned on the benefits menu as a "high deductible" choice. That accurate but arguably negative labeling focuses attention only on the deductible—the "here and now" expense. This means that inertia takes over. HSAs were established in 2003, but even after sixteen years, more than 75% of employers fail to offer their workers access to them.[8] HSAs are an opportunity for greater control over one of the biggest determinants of future income success: financing and consumption of health care today, tomorrow, and well into the future. A couple aged 65 will need $349,000 for health care costs throughout their senior years, according to a Fidelity Analysis in 2016. According to Price Waterhouse Cooper (PwC) medical care costs in 2020 are expected to rise 6%, well ahead of general inflation.

Not all health plans are HSA compatible. For 2020, the health plan must have a deductible of at least $1,400 for self-only coverage or $2,800 for family coverage and include the maximum dollars you will have to pay out of pocket.

Since medical expenses are one of the most expensive issues and notoriously difficult to try to plan around, additional thought should be put into saving for them. Many times, HSAs are available

---

8   Learning Objectives: "What's Holding Back HSAs?" co-authored by Nevin E. Adams, JD, Chief Communications Officer of the ARA; and Jack Towarnicky, Principal Researcher and sponsored by the Empower Institute, January 2020.

through 401(k) plans, but you are able to set up an HSA without being involved with a 401(k) plan. For both health insurance and savings, HSAs, in my mind, are WIN-WIN-WIN. You cannot be on Medicare and contribute to an HSA, but you can use the funds previously invested. Even Nobel laureate Richard Thaler, a behavioral economist, calls them a no-brainer!

LIFE/DISABILITY INSURANCE

Even if you have adequate health insurance, it is important to consider life and disability insurance, particularly if you are financially responsible for yourself or your family. Health insurance only covers medical expenses; if you die or you are too sick or hurt to work, it will not help pay for your mortgage or rent or put food on the table. Disability policies are intended to cover short-term medical issues that cause you to be unable to work or to work on a limited basis; life insurance policies will help cover costs if you die. Both are designed to help prevent a financial crisis for your family during emotionally troubling and stressful times. Some states automatically withdraw a small amount from each paycheck to pay for disability insurance.

LONG-TERM CARE

Not preparing for health care expenses and long-term care is one of the most common financial mistakes people make—particularly seniors preparing for the last thirty years of their lives. The Administration for Community Living recent study indicated 70% of Americans who are age 65 will need some type of long term care services, either at home, in their community, or in a facility. According to the U.S. Dept of Health and Human Services, 20% of today's 65-year-olds will need LTC for longer than 5 years. Health care costs do not decrease as we age—they increase dramatically. In addition, many current health care plans do not pay 100% for all the medical, and drug costs you are currently using.

Taking into consideration your very healthy eating habits and lifestyle, and good overall health, the aging process begins slowly to deteriorate functions; osteoporosis, just one natural aging process, may result in a fall resulting in severe bodily injury. If you are over 55 and go for a medical checkup, the first thing the nurse practitioner or physician asks is: "HAVE YOU FALLEN LATELY?"

At the turn of the twentieth century, life expectancy was 54.5 years. These days, it is not unusual for people in the industrialized world to live until age ninety-two and beyond. What are your options when your ninety-two-year-old parents are no longer able to take care of themselves or hold jobs? They may not even be ill or disabled; they may simply be unable to make a living and complete some basic functions of daily life, such as cooking and cleaning, on their own. Do you realize it would be cheaper to send them to Harvard University than it would be to send them to an assisted living center? According to the Harvard College Handbook for Students 2019–2020 for the academic year, the standard undergrad tuition at Harvard was $47,730; room and board and other fees brought this price tag to a hefty $60,659. According to a Genworth Financial 'Cost of Living Survey 2010–2018' private room nursing home cost can run $90,000 a year or more depending on the area of the country.

People are living longer than ever before, but other changes are bringing the subject of long-term care to the forefront for people of all ages. In the past, many individuals could depend on help from their families, their children, and their friends if they needed care each day. However, society is changing; it's common for children to move right after college (if not before), to live on their own, and sometimes to talk only infrequently with their parents again. People move around more and have less time or incentive to make friends in their neighborhoods or local areas. What will you do if, like Sally, you live alone and you can't go back to your parents, family, or friends for help when you can't work or even perform routine tasks?

According to the U.S. Department of Health and Human Services on their webpage longtermcare.acl.gov, the number of people who will require long-term care (whether in independent living communities, assisted living communities, Alzheimer/dementia communities, or in-home care services) is increasing and will continue to increase for the foreseeable future. In the past, you could easily get a special insurance policy to handle long-term care. It is still possible to find long-term care policies; however, most insurance companies have gotten out of this business. To get the same kind of coverage, you may need to get a hybrid insurance policy (life/annuity) that has a long-term care provision. It is best to apply for long-term care insurance while you are younger and healthier. After your mid-fifties or if you have preexisting medical conditions, you might find it difficult to find a carrier who offers a policy at a price you can afford.

MEDICAID

In reality, most people will need to rely on their own personal assets, Medicare, Medicaid, friends, and family to help them pay for and get long-term care. Sometimes family members or friends attempt to provide the care themselves. This is commendable, but can be a tremendous strain on their finances and personal lives.

Sometimes, family members who provide activities of daily living (ADL) assistance are eligible to receive reimbursement from Medicaid. These payments can help cover expenses and mitigate some of the costs involved with providing care. They are not intended to provide wages to caregivers. There are many rules that one must follow to qualify for these "cash and counseling" programs, and those rules vary state-by-state. Family members need to get training and approval as a personal care assistant (PCA). The person they are taking care of must obtain a waiver so they can use their Medicaid reimbursement payments to compensate them, and the number of waivers may be limited by the state. Some states do not permit spouses to be reimbursed for these services.

Whether you are in the position of needing or providing long-term care, meet with an attorney to draw up a formal caregiver contract and with a financial management services company to aid with the other formalities involved in the process.

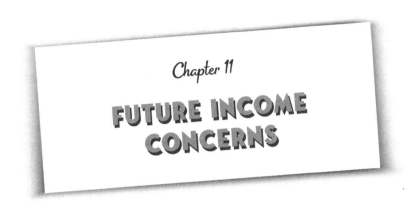

Chapter 11

FUTURE INCOME CONCERNS

*J*immy didn't graduate from college. In his second year, he was offered a job as a computer security manager at a major corporation. He wasn't passing up a once-in-a-lifetime opportunity like that, even if it meant dropping out. He received a great salary, excellent benefits, and the promise of a long and fulfilling career.

Over the next few years, Jimmy received several promotions until his salary exceeded six figures. He bought a house and put 5% (the minimum required) down. He felt he was making plenty of money, his career was running strong, and he could afford the payments. His company had a great 401(k) plan and he continued to make his monthly contributions.

His wife, Gail, worked as a dental assistant. She made good money, too, which they used to renovate their house and buy a few luxuries. They had two children, Lola and Dwayne.

One day, Jimmy and Gail watched a television show that claimed Social Security was failing and the money would soon be gone.

"Makes me wonder what we can depend on when we get into our late seventies," Jimmy said to Gail, turning off the show midway through.

"I don't know," she answered. "It brings to mind a lot of questions. Maybe we haven't been doing everything correctly."

To get the answers, they decided to talk to Rufus, an old friend who happened to be a CFP® Practitioner. Rufus had frequently expressed concern about people who did not realistically plan for future income needs.

"Good morning. It's been a while. You both doing well?" Rufus said, indicating they should sit.

"Yes, we're happy. Thanks for seeing us," Jimmy said.

"My pleasure. Are you ready to get started?"

"Sure. What do we do? We brought our records."

"Don't need those yet. First, I want to find out your goals. What are you trying to achieve?"

Jimmy explained their financial position briefly. Then, he told Rufus that he and his wife were concerned about their future income needs when they were in their seventies and beyond. They were both in good health.

"The show we watched made us afraid," Jimmy told Rufus. "Social Security has been a big part of our plans, and if it's not going to work, we need to know that now so we can do something else."

"I understand," Rufus answered. "Tell me what you're doing now."

"I have a 401(k) from my job," said Jimmy, "but Gail's job doesn't offer a plan. Other than that, we were depending on having some money from Social Security."

"The 401(k) is a good start, and you are right to be suspicious of Social Security. I don't think it's going to fail. Think of the backlash on politicians if it did! But it may certainly go through some drastic changes. It wouldn't surprise me if benefits were reduced or eligibility changed."

"So, we were right!"

"Yes, definitely. And even if nothing changes, the payouts from Social Security won't sustain the kind of lifestyle you are accustomed to or want."

"Oh, really?"

"At your pay level, you'll get a couple of thousand a month at most. Social Security is not intended to replace your current income, but rather to provide a minimum floor for living expenses."

"Seems like a small amount after working all my life."

"Yes, that's true. But the reality is that you need to change the way you think about your lifestyle in the last twenty-five to thirty years of life."

"What do you mean?"

"In the twentieth century, people would retire at sixty-seven or so, then live off their pension or other retirement fund, plus Social Security, for ten to twenty years at most. The only pension programs now are those for government workers and some unions. Every day, we hear stories of local municipalities going broke because of unfunded pension obligations. People are living longer these days. I believe you should be planning to live to 100."

"So, what do we do?" Gail asked, despair evident in her voice.

"There are a few things you can do. Of course, continue with your company's 401(k). They contribute if you contribute, which helps."

"Okay, what else?"

"Contribute to a Roth IRA."

"Good, we can do that."

"Let's come up with a long-term plan. You'll need to pay off your debts and reduce the monthly balances to allow you to pay credit card balances off each month without being charged the excessive interest rate you are paying now."

"Hopefully you'll always be healthy, but you need to plan to cover the increased medical costs you might incur as you age. If you have disability coverage at your workplace, it is most likely a group plan, usually not transferrable to an individual policy when you leave. Most who have to leave work early do so because of a medical disability."

Over the next few years, Gail and Jimmy worked towards the plan that they had devised with Rufus. In addition to their 401(k) and Roth IRA, the couple managed to squirrel away quite a bit of money in their savings—over $100,000. They both felt confident about the future.

However, Jimmy and Gail had to hit their savings time and again to pay for Lola's college education. Gail had some medical problems; she took a leave of absence to try to deal with them at first, but finally had to leave her job. They took out a second mortgage on the house to pay for the expenses that were not covered by insurance.

Their son, Dwayne, joined the military and became a career officer. Lola, on the other hand, got into an accident, which was declared to be her fault. Insurance covered the lawsuit and all its costs, including punitive damages, but she was unable to work. She had to move back home with her parents. Persistent medical bills, the cost of physical therapy, and unplanned expenses ate into the rest of their savings. Gail took a second part-time job to help make ends meet.

Jimmy continued to do well in his job, receiving promotions and raises regularly. By the time he reached sixty, his salary topped $125,000 a year. However, his boss retired and a new manager took over. He and the new manager didn't get along, so Jimmy decided to take early retirement, seven years before he'd planned.

They had $750,000 in their 401(k); $250,000 in their Roth IRA; and about $20,000 in savings. They both panicked; life changes had come quite a bit earlier than they'd expected. On the surface, that seemed like a lot of money, but Gail and Jimmy knew that they couldn't live their desired lifestyle for thirty to forty years without more income. According to their original plan, they expected to have more than double that amount in their 401(k), a much higher balance in their savings, and their house paid off.

"What do we do now?" Jimmy asked Rufus as they met at lunch.

"What are your goals, now that your employment situation has changed?" Rufus asked.

"I really don't know. It was all so sudden."

"What are you good at?"

"Computer security. I have earned multiple certifications, am well-trained, and have two decades of experience."

"How about looking for a job in computer security?"

"I could do that. You don't think being sixty years old will be a problem?"

"I think it depends on how you market yourself and how well you network. You have a lot of useful experience, knowledge, and skills. Many employers would find that extremely valuable—perhaps even more valuable than someone who has just graduated college."

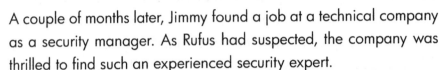

A couple of months later, Jimmy found a job at a technical company as a security manager. As Rufus had suspected, the company was thrilled to find such an experienced security expert.

Gail enjoyed working with flowers and in the garden, so she started her own little company selling exotic orchids and other flowers from a stand at the local shopping mall. At first, she'd hesitated about approaching the mall, but they thought her idea was fantastic. She didn't need a lot of space, she supplied her own cart, and her business added a bit of local flair to the shopping experience. The mall management even helped her with the permits and licenses she needed and gave her a break on the commission they charged for the space.

Within a year, both Jimmy and Gail were happily working in new careers they loved. They were making a good income, and the thought of retiring vanished from their minds. Their new plan was to remain busily employed, either in their own business ventures or working for someone else, until they could no longer work.

SOCIAL SECURITY

Social Security was signed into law in 1935 under President Franklin D. Roosevelt and began in 1937. At the time, most working people had pension funds and their own savings—Social Security payments were supposed to be the "frosting" on the cake. Today, the only thing remaining for most Americans is the frosting. (Note: Government workers have a pension system which does not correspond to the modern options for those outside the government.) Congress passes laws for itself which do not apply to us. After the Affordable Care Act was passed in March 2010, Congress opted out for themselves. Personally, I believe Congress should have the same "retirement" options available to most workers—IRAs or 401(k)—no pension. I also believe we should pass a constitutional amendment for term limits for Congress. But I digress.

The rumors of the mishandling of Social Security funds has been going on since the mid-1980s. According to an article published by *Money Watch* "3 Big Myths About Social Security," *Social Security is not insurance or an investment in the conventional sense, where the amount of benefits you receive is directly related to the amount of money you invest via your FICA taxes.*

Senator Russell Long, a lifelong supporter of Social Security, explains it this way: *Social Security is nothing more than a promise to a group of people that their children will be taxed for that group's benefit.*

Are you OK with the idea of paying your FICA taxes to fund the Social Security benefits for your parents? The *Money Watch* article goes on to ask the question you may be asking: "What's the appropriate amount of taxes that our government needs to take to pay for Social Security from workers who are struggling to just meet daily living expenses? And what's the appropriate level of benefits needed to support our senior citizens?"

In my opinion, the Social Security structure needs to be changed, either through starting benefits later, changing benefit amounts, or a combination of both.

One of the most basic postulates of Western civilization is that there are more younger people active in the workforce than there are older people who are no longer working. Social Security is based on this assumption—that the younger workforce will contribute to Social Security and support those who have left the workforce after reaching the "magic" age.

The problem with this assumption is that it's no longer valid. Medical advances are allowing people to live longer; in fact, it's very possible that life spans will increase beyond 100 years in the very near future. In the Western world, the rate of population growth is also slowing. According to the US Census Bureau, in 2015, 2.2 million people were added to the population of the United States, bringing the total to 323 million people. That's an increase of only 0.7%, which is the smallest yearly increase since 1937. Historically it's grown much faster, as much as 1.8% per year (Chokshi, 2016).

That might seem like a good thing. After all, isn't overpopulation one of the problems that the world faces? If the population continues to increase, won't we run out of living space before too long?

In fact, while it is true that overpopulation is a problem, the declining rate of population growth is producing changes in society and economics that are dramatically affecting individuals, families, and the workplace. Fewer people means fewer workers, which means fewer tax dollars for the federal government. This puts Social Security and Medicare at risk, because those programs assume a large working base to subsidize older, nonworking people. As life expectancy increases, these programs will be under increased financial pressure to remain solvent. On the other hand, because slowed population growth may result in fewer people in the workplace, competition for jobs may decline, resulting in it becoming easier to find employment if you are properly trained with the skills required for the modern workplace. The housing market is also helped, since there will be fewer people competing for available units (Hagenbaugh, 2004).

The most visible effect of slowing population growth will be on Social Security and Medicare benefits and expansion of those programs. Your financial plans must consider that these programs probably won't be enough to sustain your standard of living in your older years. In many cases, they may not be adequate today.

Social Security, according to the latest studies, is solvent only until 2033 because of demographic pressures and the previously weak economy over the past decade. Most Americans feel it is a vital program and extremely important for older generations. However, it is possible benefits will be reduced or payroll taxes increased to ensure the system remains viable. The most likely change will be an increase in the age to receive full benefits. This change has already begun. (Frankel, 2017)

The world is changing very quickly because of these and other trends. Because of that, traditional financial planning, with built-in concepts such as retirement and what withdrawal percentage is reasonable, may not be realistic. Social Security and Medicare may not be sufficient for your family to have adequate financial support or medical coverage. Medicare does not pay for routine medical tests. Eye refraction, a test most seniors need, is an example of a routine medical test. This is the test where you look at a chart and the technician asks which is better, #1 or #2, and the results determine your need for eyeglasses or adjustment to your current eyeglass prescription.

We are living into our late nineties, so the focus of the word "senior" should also adjust, possibly to age 78+. Our government also should consider adjusting its definition of "retirement age." Age 75 to 76 would be a more realistic starting point for reducing full time work. The public, however, would be outraged if the government made these changes without phasing them in. The 2019 Retirement SECURE ACT (**S**etting **E**very **C**ommunity **U**p for **R**etirement **E**nhancement) has updated the life expectancy tables and is gradually increasing the starting age for RMD withdrawals to age 72-1/2. The law also allows annuities to be added to employer 401(k) accounts to help provide participants with "lifetime" income options, as a pension model used to provide. These investment options are available today outside of a 401(k) plan—another good reason to work with a financial coach.

SAVINGS AND INVESTMENTS

In lieu of relying on Social Security, we must explore other sources of financial stability and future income sources for the later years of our lives.

SAVINGS

As we've already discussed, one of your primary financial SMART goals should be to build up the cost of a *minimum* six months of expenses in your savings account. The best way to build up your savings is to get in the habit of depositing a certain amount from each paycheck or other funds that you receive. The ideal amount is *20% of the gross check*, but if you can't do that, then save what you can and increase the amount as your situation improves. Start with 1%.

Since medical expenses are one of the most expensive issues and notoriously difficult to try to plan around, additional thought should be put into saving for them.

Finally, with HSAs (Health Savings Account), you never have to worry about spending all your money by a certain deadline. Unlike Flexible Spending Accounts (FSAs), which have similar tax benefits but require you to use contributed money or forfeit it on an annual basis, Health Savings Accounts let you carry forward unused balances indefinitely. The accounts are also portable to your next employer. That can give you the confidence you want that your money will be there when you really need it. If you stick to the spirit of why you set up the HSA in the first place, then the upfront deduction and tax-free income combine to be a powerful savings tool that no other tax-favored account today can match.

FUTURE INCOME ACCOUNTS

The government has created several different ways for you to save money for *the future*. Even though the concept of retirement in my professional assessment, is becoming less and less *realistic* as the modern era progresses, society and businesses are still structured to support the concept. You can use this to your advantage to build up future income sources, since the government incentivizes these options.

Of course, the first thing that comes to mind when we speak of future income is Social Security (the government's pension plan to which we contribute in our working years). Of course, that should be part of your financial plan for your future—hopefully it will be available. It is money that the government has taken from your paychecks and saved for you after you reach 62, 65, 67, 70, or 72 years of age. Unfortunately, the amount of money that you will get on a monthly basis from Social Security is relatively small and won't support your lifestyle for the most part. However, it will be an income source for you in your senior years.

Many companies provide access to a 401(k) or IRA plans as a benefit for their employees and also contribute *extra money* to your account *just for showing up to work each day*. Discuss these plans in detail with your financial coach and your company's HR department to ensure that you understand the options.

401(k) plans came into existence in 1980. By 1982, the stock market was having a boom period, and as a result, account values increased quickly. They were set up as supplemental accounts—a third tier to supplement the basic pension plans of the day along with Social Security. Individuals were allowed to make their own investment decisions and even decide if they wanted to participate in a 401(k). The old-fashioned pensions have almost disappeared, resulting in the 401(k) plan, which was sort of supplementary, now being almost everybody's basic plan. People started with one kind of pension system, in which all the decisions were made for them and they were guaranteed income for as long as they were going to live, and they ended up with a completely different system.

I believe the government needs to lift the dollar restrictions on the amount of money that can be contributed to these "retirement" plans on an annual basis. Regular IRA/401(k) contributions are pre-income tax, reducing the amount of annual income taxes collected by the government. By restricting the dollar amount a worker can contribute, less taxes are collected currently but the government is assured of collecting income taxes in the future. Why should good savers be penalized for wanting to save more money?

With the regular IRA or 401(k), you receive an income tax deduction when you make the original investment, but you must pay income tax when the government requires you to start taking distributions, and the latest age to start withdrawals as of 2020 is age 72 1/2. You will pay income tax on the original investment as well as the growth within the account. Income taxes are usually the highest tax we as individuals pay. My personal preference is a ROTH account because with a ROTH account I will pay taxes on the seeds rather than the crop.

Say you are 75 years old. A $400,000 401(k) account divided by 24.6 (or 4.07% of your account balance) equals a required minimum distribution of $16,260. This amount and your Social Security payment would both be income-taxable. Each year the percentage you need to withdraw from your retirement 401(k) account grows larger because the government wants it taxed prior to your death. At age 80, the percentage you need to withdraw is 5.3%; your life expectancy at this point, according to the government, is 18.7 years. This is one of the reasons people are running out of money before they run out of time.

More troubling, according to data provided by the IRS, of the Americans who are required to take distributions from retirement 401(k) or IRA accounts, only roughly 20% are taking the minimum required. The remaining 80% are taking more than the required minimum, thus increasing the withdrawal starting age and making any decreases in RMDs a moot point.

A Roth IRA/401(k) is a wonderful option—I believe the ROTH should be the preferred savings vehicle for most individuals. The government could encourage use of ROTH investments by allowing twice the contribution allowed in a regular 401(k) or IRA. The government would be happy, because they get their tax money up front, and the individual would be able to increase savings for future income needs. With a ROTH 401(k) or ROTH IRA, you will pay the taxes now, but the money will grow tax deferred. When you take it out, it will be tax free, and the government does not require you to withdraw it at a specific age because you have already paid the taxes. Why not pay the tax on the seeds rather than on the crop? Some companies have both tax-deferred as well as Roth options. If not, you may be able to open your own Roth IRA and make additional contributions to it.

In 2006, Congress made it easier for employers to enroll workers automatically in 401(k) plans and invest their money in what are called "target date funds." These funds shift focus from stocks to bonds as people age. Unfortunately, requiring an employer to provide Roth 401(k)s as well as regular 401(k)s was not part of the law. Target date funds move a larger portion of the investment to more conservative income options and out of equities as the participant gets closer to "retirement" age of 65. In my professional assessment, this time-table is not realistic because we are living longer and need to have more growth well into our late 70s. Again, retirement is an outdated concept; I believe more growth is needed later in life.

What you're really doing when you contribute to an IRA is investing in stocks or bonds within a mutual fund (MF) or exchange-traded fund (ETF).[9] You should discuss these company plans with your financial coach, who can help you make the choices appropriate for your risk tolerance and goals.

INVESTMENTS

Before you consider starting an investment account, pay off all of your credit cards. It doesn't make sense for an investment to earn you 10% on your money when you're paying 20% or even 30% on the money you have charged on your credit cards.

There are many different investments available to you. Two of the most common categories are:

- **Stocks**—When you purchase stocks, you're basically buying a piece of a company. By being a shareholder, you own part of that company. Some stocks issue dividends (profits). The value of your shares can go up or down over time depending upon the value of the company.

- **Bonds**—By purchasing bonds, you are loaning money to a private corporation or the government. Typically, government bonds are used to fund large projects such as schools, highways, canals, and so forth. Treasury bonds are used to help fund the federal government. Corporate bonds

---

9 Mutual funds (MFs) and exchange-traded funds (ETFs) are sold by prospectus. Please consider the investment objectives, risks, charges, and expenses carefully before investing. The prospectus, which contains this and other information about the investment company, can be obtained from the fund company or your financial professional. Be sure to read the prospectus carefully before deciding whether to invest.

may be used for company expansion or acquisitions. In general, bonds may have a relatively low rate of return vs. stock market returns, but they tend to be considered safer than most other investment methods as long as the company has a good financial rating. The amount of interest that the company will usually have to pay is in some ways dependent on their credit rating. The higher the credit rating (AAA, AA, BBB, etc.), the less interest the corporation will need to pay to entice buyers. You and I have the same situation when we go to the bank to borrow money. The better our credit rating (credit score), the lower the interest charge the bank will require from us. We should continue to monitor corporate financials whether we own bonds or stock in a company. Recently we have seen stores as large as Sears Roebuck, Toys "R" Us, and Brookstone declare bankruptcy.

Once you've got credit cards paid off and at least 6 months in savings, it's time to start thinking about longer-term investments. Many individual investment account opportunities are available; these include everything from stocks to bonds. A good strategy for the future is to have a *balanced portfolio*. This serves as a buffer if one or two investments have a negative return. Exchange-traded funds, mutual funds, and individual stocks and bonds are all available, and each provides differing opportunities. A financial coach can provide you with insights as to which ones would be appropriate for your goals and risk tolerance. This is another area where "do-it-yourself" on the internet may not be your best option.

ONLINE COMMERCE

The changes in the world around us over the past few decades have shifted nearly every aspect of life—particularly financial life. As the world continues to change, it's important for us to understand what is happening, so we know what benefits we can draw from it and what we can do to grow our financial stability throughout our entire lives.

Cash in the modern era is a topic discussed in depth by David D. Friedman and Kerry L. Macintosh. They indicate we live in a world of monopoly monies in two senses. First, most people find it convenient to use the same money as their neighbors; thus, money is usually a geographic monopoly. Second, nations have found it profitable to seize control over the money presses. As a result, the geographic monopoly is generally held by the money issued by the government that rules that particular piece of geography. The end result is familiar to us all: Americans use dollars; Japanese use yen; Britons use pounds; and so forth.

As we move through modern times, online commerce and electronic money will continue to grow in importance. These and other technological developments will undermine money monopolies and increase the likelihood that systems of competing moneys—both public and private—will emerge. Electronic money will produce changes to our payment systems; digital currencies have already begun to emerge. Digital currency is a type of currency available in digital form. It exhibits properties similar to physical currencies, but can allow for instantaneous transactions and borderless transfer-of-ownership. Examples include virtual currencies and cryptocurrencies (e.g., Bitcoins).

According to Friedman and Macintosh, technology will affect money in the following ways:

(1) the internet and online commerce; (2) computers that can perform complex calculations; (3) electronic currency that is easy to create, manage and redeem; and (4) increased bandwidth leading to real-time audio and video.

Each factor will play a role in determining the future of money—and the future of money plays a large role in all of our individual futures.

Chapter 12

PLANNING FOR CONSTANT CHANGE

*R*honda had a great job as a travel agent, but she had more and more trouble finding work after everyone started turning to the internet to plan and arrange their own trips. She was already feeling down when a hurricane ripped through her community and destroyed the home she and her husband had lived in since they day they'd gotten back from their honeymoon. The stress tore apart their marriage, and after a bad divorce and some terrible financial choices, Rhonda was in dire financial ruin. She'd lost her home, her car, and everything else she knew. She literally owned nothing except the clothes on her back, a few dollars in her purse, and a pair of shoes.

Although depressed and anxious about her situation, fortunately, unlike many people she knew, Rhonda didn't have any addictions to deal with. Her mother had died from an overdose, and Rhonda had taken that to be a sign from G-d that she shouldn't use drugs or drink to excess.

She had to ask a friend if she could stay with her for a few weeks until she could recover, but those weeks turned into months. Rhonda's friends were happy to help her in her time of difficulty, but

Rhonda didn't want to be a burden on anyone. She tried her hardest to provide whatever she could for herself.

One morning as she was walking to the local soup kitchen, Rhonda felt someone come up behind her and push her aside. Hands grabbed her purse and pulled it from her shoulder. She spun around, but the young man was too fast; he got away with her purse.

That was the last straw.

A week later, she borrowed some clean clothes from a friend, and put in an application to a temp agency. Soon, she was working small jobs. She was a good bookkeeper, a fast learner, and highly motivated.

One company liked her so much, they offered her a part-time position, and she accepted. Within a month, Rhonda had saved up enough to start paying her friend rent.

Within six months, she had saved enough to move into a small studio apartment within walking distance of her job. It wasn't great and she had only a bed, but it was her own place.

"I don't know what to do now," Rhonda confessed to her friend Sue. "I'm making enough for the rent and food, but I want a car. Taking the bus everywhere is driving me crazy."

"I understand. Let me ask you, do you track your expenses and income?"

"What do you mean?"

"Do you know how much you need to pay your expenses each week versus how much you spend?"

"Oh, you mean a budget?"

"No, not a budget . . . just a list of what you spend and what the essentials cost—rent, utilities, food, etc."

"I see. No, I haven't done that."

"Here's some homework, then. Make a list of your spending as you go through the next month. Don't make any changes to your habits, just list everything. When we get back together, we'll go through it together and see where you can make changes."

Rhonda made a list of everything she spent over the next month, and she and Sue went over what she'd done.

"Okay, the amount you spend on groceries seems high. I think you could find a cheaper store and maybe use coupons to lower the cost of what you buy."

"Sure, there's a discount store just down the road."

"Why don't you shop there?"

"I don't know. I'm just used to the other store."

"Well, how about switching? I'll bet you save a lot of money."

The two went over the rest of the list and came up with over a dozen other suggestions that would save Rhonda over $200 a month.

"You said your goal is a car?" asked Sue. "Do you need a car, or do you want a car because it's more convenient?"

"No, I need a car."

"That's a nice goal," Sue responded. "What do you want over the longer term?"

"Get a bigger place and have enough money so everything isn't an emergency."

"What do you like to do? Like, what are your hobbies and such?"

"Oh . . . well, I know this will sound weird, but I like to cook, and I love to make different kinds of drinks—you know, margaritas and things like that."

"Why don't you turn that into a second job?"

"Hey! That's right! I could get my bartender's license and work in a bar. Good money there."

Rhonda took Sue's advice and earned a bartender's license. She found a second job quickly, working in a nice bar downtown from her studio apartment. She worked a lot of hours between her two jobs, but it felt good to be supporting herself again. All the bad thoughts from her past that had been weighing her down faded away.

As it turned out, Rhonda loved bartending. She'd always been fascinated by people, a natural-born people watcher, and bartending gave her plenty of opportunities. She enjoyed experimenting with different recipes for cocktails, and word of her drink concoctions spread quickly around town. She got noticed by a local reporter, who wrote her story in a popular magazine. Because of this story, the bar became a local hotspot, with people coming from miles around just to sample Rhonda's drinks and see her work. She even signed a few autographs!

PLANNING FOR CONSTANT CHANGE

The future of life in America and around the developed world is undergoing rapid and tremendous change.

Technology is a part of our everyday lives. The internet has provided each of us with opportunities to investigate everything from how to make a great hamburger to how to brush our teeth properly. There is an endless supply of knowledge. However, we should not forget that we are humans, not machines, and we do need contact with other humans. Reading articles alone will not provide us with the insights and knowledge we individually need.

One of the most significant trends that's already causing massive changes in manufacturing, business, and the economy is automation. Entire industries are in the process of being automated, eliminating the need for many workers. Whole factories are being filled with robots to build machines such as automobiles, ships, and just about anything else imaginable. These buildings are empty of people except for a few supervisory personnel and some technicians.

Even computer rooms are changing. Big companies have had large amounts of real estate set aside for their corporate computers. These rooms required technical support from highly-trained people. However, in the modern era, these specialized rooms are being replaced by truck-sized modules that are sealed and never opened after they are delivered. If the computers inside the room fail, the entire room is replaced.

Many of the new ships planned for the future are designed to operate without a crew. Even the large cranes that handle shipping containers will be replaced with robots. You've all heard of automated cars that are coming very soon, but do you know that fully automated trucks are already beginning to hit the road? In the not-too-distant future, entire convoys of dozens of trucks will drive the freeways completely driverless. The jobs of millions of truck drivers will be changing because of this trend. Automobile technicians will be replaced by email update notifications to your automobile computer, just as our cell phones and personal computers are currently updated. You will determine by a click of a button when you want the update to be installed. Hardware will continue to break (just as it does with computers and phones), but many of the tasks we have long considered routine maintenance will be extinct.

Robotics and Artificial Intelligence (AI) will be some of the faster-growing trends in business throughout the modern era. They will most likely play an increasing role in senior health care, allowing people to remain in their homes with robots or drones doing tasks that people can physically no longer do on their own.

All these automated systems might sound like science fiction, but most of them are already being implemented. These trends are important because they will affect all industries everywhere in one way or another. Just as we have already seen various outdated occupations, like the travel agent, milkman, or VCR repairman shift or disappear altogether, the entire workforce will undergo massive changes as tasks can be better performed by robotic, automated systems.

Just thinking about these changes can be overwhelming, and it can seem as if there's nothing you can do to be ready for them. Obviously, it's impossible to know exactly where the future is headed. However, there are trends that can be predicted and others that will pop up seemingly out of the blue. Our future world will depend more on our dreams and visions than our current knowledge.

The truth of the matter is that by understanding the changes that are happening, you can adjust your skill set through education, ensure you have adequate financial depth to weather changes, and make wise choices about your future. Thus, it's important for you, as you plan your financial future, to build in flexibility. Subscribe to the trade journals of your industry and keep up to date with what's going on; continually keep yourself trained to improve your marketability. Ensure you have enough financial depth so that when your circumstances change, you can make a move to a different job, industry, or career without it being a crisis. You can come out ahead and live an even happier and healthier life.

Technology is just one of many changes that are and will continue to affect us in the years to come. Whether you believe global warming is a fact or a fiction created by environmental special interests, it's obvious that the weather is changing. Storms are becoming larger and of longer duration, droughts are occurring throughout the world, and rainfall patterns are changing in unpredictable ways.

Peter Ticktin, founder of The Global Warming Foundation, sees the effects of Earth's temperature rising exponentially. He says that this is not in our grandchildren's or even our children's lifetimes, but rather in our time on the planet. That these changes are already easily discernable—for example, he shows that our storms carry more water more regularly. Hurricane Harvey dropped more than four feet of rainwater on Houston, and we have seen five feet of rain drop on Hawaii and Taiwan in recent years. In 2009, Typhoon Morakot dropped over nine feet of rain on Taiwan. Imagine that!

Peter suggests that we should watch the small things in our own backyards. For instance, he believes that as we progress, there will be more and more air travel interruptions and problems with our ground infrastructure. Different regions will see different changes. Some, for instance will see more extreme floods, which cause more deaths.

Changing climate and weather patterns are a natural part of the Earth's evolution. However, global warming causes climate change to act faster than it should. Understanding changing weather conditions is essential to the long-term planning of your financial future and your life. Living in a warm climate such as Florida may provide personal living benefits, but the location of your home may be at risk due to rising sea levels or larger storms, such as hurricanes, and the cost of insuring it will be higher than other areas.

Obviously, all areas of the world are affected by the weather. However, some locations tend to get harsher weather and are more likely to experience detrimental changes. Take the time to confront what's happening with weather in the area where you are living. Large portions of the city of New Orleans, for instance, are below sea level, being kept dry only by levees and massive pumps. Major hurricanes such as Katrina can overwhelm even the best-built seawalls and levees and cause massive flooding. The scenic route up the coast of California is lined with homes built directly in the path of mudslides. Every time it rains, these homes are in danger, and every year the news is filled with reports and videos of buildings that have been undermined or buried by a landslide. Due to an unusually dry 2018, California had the worst fire in its history; entire towns were devastated, and many lost their lives. In the summer of 2020, fires consumed more than 4 million acres, and will surpass the destruction caused by the fires of 2018. California has passed laws to reduce the risk of megafires through forest management, however, the funds for these projects have frequently been sidelined.

Don't be afraid of climate change. Instead, become educated about the weather and other natural phenomena such as earthquakes or floods in your area or the location where you plan to buy a house. Include the weather in your planning for your finances and your future, and choose to live in an area where you're not constantly threatened by natural phenomena. Yes, climate change is a natural phenomenon; however, living in close proximity to the coastline or on the banks of a river creates an added risk. If you choose to live in an area that may be at risk, ensure that you plan contingencies for potential disasters and emergencies (possibly an extra 5 or 6 months of savings in your emergency fund).

RISKS AND HOW TO MITIGATE THEM

The goal for people from the moment they reach adulthood has long been to achieve financial success. However, it is important to consider the entirety of our lives: each consists of many sunny, rainy, and unexpectedly windy days. Good financial principles consider today *and* tomorrow, and they contain some umbrellas to protect us. Assessing your local area will help you determine what kinds of insurances you need to purchase.

Life changes. It's always best to expect the unexpected and plan for emergencies and expenditures. Significant unplanned events can quickly burn through savings and even force you to eat into your investments if you don't have a plan in place to handle them.

Disasters that can occur include:

- Natural events such as earthquakes, hurricanes, tsunamis, other storms, and wildfires and pandemics.

- Fire and smoke damage to your house.

- Criminal activities such as theft, mugging, a home invasion, or someone stealing your car.

A host of other unexpected emergencies or disasters can also occur, including health and disability issues (which we will explore further when we meet Sally), or professionally-based legal issues (which we will talk about when we meet Linda). How do you plan for events that, by their nature, can't be planned for? Professional athletes know that disability can occur early in their careers and they need to be prepared.

Insurance policies are how we try to anticipate these unexpected expenses.[10] They can help you with losses or problems that occur after an emergency or disaster. These policies are not only beneficial, they are frequently required—auto insurance is legally mandated in many states, renters' insurance is usually a requirement of apartment complexes, and homeowners' insurance is necessary to purchase and finance a house. Every one of these will be invaluable if a covered problem occurs; conversely, living without the appropriate insurance policies can lead to financial disaster.

---

10 Insurance policies are issued by insurance companies to cover unexpected events. If an event happened consistently, an insurance company would not issue a policy to cover its occurrence. Insurance policies vary by state laws.

For your home, you are typically required by a lienholder (usually the bank that provides the mortgage) to purchase a certain amount of homeowners' insurance. It's a good idea to carry this type of insurance regardless of whether or not it's required, because the policy will cover damage to your home. Note that in some states, such as California, earthquake insurance must be bought separately; on other states, such as Ohio, flood insurance is also purchased separately. According to FEMA (Federal Emergency Management Agency), flooding is the number one natural disaster in the United States as well as the costliest.

If you are a renter, you can acquire renters' insurance to cover losses that occur to your possessions within your apartment. Most apartment complexes require renters' insurance from their tenants. Additionally, you can also purchase coverage for short-term living expenses if your apartment is rendered unlivable.

If you own a car, your state probably requires you to purchase certain amounts of automobile insurance. Your lienholder (the bank that loaned you the money for the car) may also require this type of insurance to protect their interests. Automobile insurance differs from state to state, and it is best to discuss the details with your insurance agent.

There are many other types of insurance policies available, and you should work with insurance agents to determine which ones are best for your needs. Additionally, it's a good idea to have a long discussion with your insurance agent so you understand each policy you are considering. Sometimes the wording can be very difficult to understand for the uninitiated, because the details are usually in "legalese."

By carefully choosing insurance policies and purchasing what you need without going overboard, you can protect yourself and your family from unexpected expenses caused by emergencies or lawsuits. As your income and/or expenses increase, you may need to adjust the policy limits. Again, a professional in this area will be able to provide you with specific guidance for your situation. This is one of the many financial and medical areas of life where do-it-yourself action is not usually in your best interest.

PRIORITIZING FINANCES

Sometimes life can throw you a curve ball, and everything seems to melt down. Everyone has curve balls; how we handle them makes the difference. Making sure you are properly insured will go a long way, but it won't help you regain everything. What do you do when you don't seem to have any choices? There is always hope, and you can turn things around—if you take control instead of letting life control you.

Sometimes, no matter how bad it gets, you can get stuck in a rut that becomes comfortable because it's familiar. That lasts until something happens to force you out of your rut. It could be you are stuck in a job you hate, a marriage that isn't working, or a school that doesn't work for you. As with Rhonda, you could even become more or less homeless. Change is intimidating and frightening, so you remain in your rut.

Even if you were born into poverty or find yourself homeless or unemployed, you can find a way to change your circumstances. It may not be easy and you may need the help of friends, your church, or others, but there's always a way as long as you take control instead of letting life control you.

Many people don't have goals, at least not consciously. They just live from day to day and don't think about tomorrow very much. Sometimes money is so tight, there doesn't appear to be a way out, and dreams become quashed in the harshness of reality. It's very difficult to think of tomorrow when you don't have the money to eat today—but if you want something different, it's crucial to understand where you are. It's the only way to make good decisions about where you want to go.

One of the best places to start when trying to get control of your finances is taking a look at what you spend. If you're like most people, you spend a lot of money without really thinking about it. For example, it's quite common for employees to go to the local fast food chain or restaurant to eat. It's easier (or so they think) than making a lunch in the morning and bringing it to work. Did you go out to lunch today? How much did that meal out cost you? If you went to an actual sit-down restaurant, it was probably on the order of $10 to $12 plus tip. Sometimes it might even be $20 plus tip. A Big Mac meal is $4.99. Add bacon and extra sauce and the price is $6.50. If you eat there three times a week for a month, that's $75.00 just for lunch.

To keep it simple, let's assume you spend $10 per day, five days a week on lunch. That means in a week, you're spending $50, and in a month, you're spending $200. That's $200, or probably more, that could have been spent on a car payment, saved in your emergency fund, or used to pay off debt. To put it another way, that's $200 gone without giving you any significant return for your money other than a few extra calories you would prefer not to have.

You could make your own lunch, bring it to work, and store it in the office refrigerator. That will probably cost you $2 to $4, or $40 to $80 a month. You can be social with the gang one day a week rather than every day. You may even discover new friends who also bring their lunches to work.

We've covered just paying for lunch. Think about the expenses associated with buying a cup of coffee at the local Starbucks every morning before going to work. At $2 to $3 for plain coffee (more per cup for fancy coffee), you've easily spent another $100 in a month. To put that in perspective, making a cup of coffee at home costs maybe $0.20. Cutting that trip to Starbucks out of your day saves you $40 to $60.

The problem with these kinds of expenses is that you don't think about them. After all, getting a cup of coffee at Starbucks costs only $2, and eating lunch at the local fast food restaurant costs only $10. That doesn't seem like a lot of money. But if you add up the total cost over a yearlong period, you can see that you're spending between $3,000 and $4,000 just purchasing a cup of coffee and lunch each workday.

Do you understand where your money goes each week? Do you know what you spend your money on and why? For a week or two, just write down everything you purchase in a journal or note it on your phone. You can dictate the item and its cost into your phone. Don't make any evaluations as to whether or not you need it, and don't change any of your spending. Just track everything. Yes, everything. At the end of that week or two, take a look at your journal. You'll probably be shocked at how much money you spend on things you didn't really need.

This exercise alone could result in savings of thousands of dollars per year that could be used to get out of debt and to build up your emergency savings.

Chapter 13

NEW PATHS

*L*inda wanted to be a scientist. Her desire began when she was twelve and Santa Claus left her a home chemistry set. Linda spent many happy days experimenting, all while imagining she was working in a top-secret lab. She even wore a white lab coat, held a magnifying glass, and frequently looked into her microscope. Her imagination ran rampant as her chemicals fizzed, boiled, and bubbled.

Unfortunately, Linda's budding career as a chemist was cut short after she almost caught her hair on fire and blew up the garage. Her chemicals were confiscated by her parents, who threw them in the garbage.

"Mom, I'll be more careful! I promise!"

"I know you love chemistry, but it's too dangerous for a thirteen-year-old. I'm sorry, but the chemistry set has to go."

"Okay, Mom," Linda replied sullenly.

"How about a nice baking set? You know, the one with the little oven you can use to make cakes and candies?"

"A baking set? Really? Mom!" Linda replied, disappointed. What would she do with a baking set? She couldn't make it fizz, explode, or catch fire—what use was it?

"Cheer up, you little mad scientist," her mom replied, almost as if she were reading Linda's mind.

Linda decided to try something different. "How about a hamster?"

"A hamster? What are you going to do with one of those ugly little rodents?"

"Hamsters are cool! I'll feed it and pet it and love it!"

"Okay, okay. How can I resist that smile? Sure, we'll get you a hamster . . . and a baking set."

Linda stuffed the baking set in the closet unused for nearly three months. One day, though, she was bored, so she finally took the set out of the box, assembled it, and started making a cake. It wasn't very good, but baking did remind her of mixing the chemicals in her beloved chemistry set. Linda finally realized that excellent baking was all about the chemistry of the ingredients—chemistry in the kitchen.

Before long, Linda was making tiny little cookies, cakes, and tasty candies for all her friends. She even started a bake stand in the front yard during the summer to make a little extra money.

Within a year, Linda took over the baking duties for the household, especially for holidays, making cookies, cakes, and even homemade candy and ice cream for family and friends.

In college, Linda met Joseph; they got married and raised five children together. Linda loved kids, and five seemed to be the ideal number.

One of her children, Richard, was diagnosed with autism when he was six. When he entered school, the counselors insisted that he start psychiatric medication. They didn't seem to care that the child was well-adjusted and had excellent grades. He had autism, so that meant he needed drugs; that's what their manual said, so that's what they were going to do.

"I'm very upset," Linda complained to Joseph.

"Are there alternatives?" he asked.

"No. They made it clear that to remain in public school, he must be drugged."

"What about private school?"

"Too expensive. You know we don't have the money for that."

"True. I was reading about this thing called homeschooling. What about that?"

A week later, Linda pulled her children from public school and began teaching them at home. She taught lessons every day to all her kids and made sure their curriculum was challenging and varied.

"We need to send them back to public school," Linda told her husband one day.

"Why?" he asked.

"They've got to learn how to interact with other children in a social environment. They can't do that at home."

"Okay. If that's what you want, let's send them to school."

He noticed that his wife looked a little sad. "I take it you really don't want to send them back to school?"

"I do. It's for their own good. I just enjoy having children around all the time. I like teaching. I don't know what else to do with myself."

"Well, you like to bake, don't you?"

"Um, yes, I do."

"So, how about opening a bakery? Kids would come by every day to get treats, and you'd make cookies and cakes and everything they love. You could even teach classes on baking, healthy eating, and stuff like that."

"That sounds cool! But, how would we afford it?"

"I don't know, but our friend Rosanna started a business of her own. Maybe we can talk to her and get some advice."

"Sure. Set up a time, and let's see what Rosanna has to say. After all, what is there to lose?"

A few days later, Linda visited Rosanna. It was kind of frightening having to tell someone else about her finances. Linda and her husband had never opened up about their bills, mortgage, taxes, and income to anyone except their accountant before.

"Hi, Linda," Rosanna said, giving her friend a big hug. "How have you been?"

"Very good, thanks. I hope you can help. I want to start my own baking business."

"Good! I'd love to help! Tell me about your passions and goals."

Linda spent the next hour talking about her love for children, her joy of baking, her passion for science, and how she'd homeschooled her kids.

"I want to be part of the community and help children," she said, "and start a business. I think a small bakery would be great, but I'm clueless when it comes to figuring out how to finance it. I have some credit cards—"

Rosanna interrupted her at this point. "Don't even think about financing your business on credit cards."

"Why not?"

"The interest rates alone will eat you alive, and it's doubtful that you'll make enough, at least in the first couple of years, to pay them off. If you buy on credit, you are purchasing money, and you must pay it back later—plus interest. When you purchase something on a card with a 22% interest rate, and if you pay the minimum each month and charge more, it can take twenty years to pay off the balance."

"Wow, I didn't know that. It doesn't sound very smart."

"There are times it makes sense to purchase on credit. For example, purchasing on a card offering zero percent interest for eighteen months is okay if you pay it off in that time. Most people think they'll pay it back, but something comes up and they don't—and then they get stuck with the high interest."

"Oh. Well, how do I get the money?"

"First, we need to talk about how much you need. You say you want a small shop on Main Street?"

"Yes, that would be perfect. Lots of foot traffic."

"Do you understand the costs involved?"

"Well . . ."

"Equipment, insurance, the shop rent itself, promotion, marketing, supplies—it all adds up to quite a sum. Plus, you'll need to get permitting."

"Oh, I hadn't realized . . ."

"How about starting your bakery in your home? You know, make cakes and cookies and other treats and deliver them. By starting small, you can build your business using the profits you make."

"That's an idea. I have a large kitchen that's fully equipped."

"Good. Let's create a business plan. This is important. You need to understand the costs, potential profits, how much you need to invest, and your options for various contingencies. If you did decide to get a loan from the bank or a small business loan from the government, you'll need that anyway."

"That sounds like a good idea."

"Once you've got that, you'll know how much money you need, when you need it, and how you're going to earn it back."

"Good. Let's go for it. I don't want it to be hugely complicated. That's why my husband and I chose a bakery—it's not difficult. Sure, there's complexity, and I may need to get the proper licensing and permitting, but I can do that."

"Yes, you're right. You'll need permits and inspections. But you can write off part of your home as a business expense on your taxes."

"Great! As far as supplies, I'm sure there are websites that will list what I need."

"Sure. So, that's your homework. Figure out what you need to start your business: all the equipment, supplies, business license, permits, insurance, and so on. Also, look at your money and see if you can fund it from what you already have instead of using credit."

"Great! I can do that!"

"I know you can. Buy me lunch in, say, a week? We'll talk more."

Over the next few weeks, Linda and her husband worked with Rosanna to create an excellent business plan. After reviewing their assets, they decided they didn't need any credit to start their business. They used a small part of their savings to get the insurance, permits, and equipment needed.

Linda's bakery quickly became popular throughout the town for its excellent cakes and other goodies. Within two years, Linda rented a small shop on Main Street in a well-trafficked area near the schools. Linda gave a free cookie to any child who came into the shop, so she had a steady stream of youngsters visiting all day long.

Linda donated 10% of each sale to help disadvantaged children in her community; in time, her bake shop became famous not just for her tasty cakes, but also because she always gave back to children and to the community. In other words, she went the extra mile and grew her business into more than just another bakery; it became part of the lives of everyone who lived in her town.

Five years later, Linda looked back on what she and her husband had accomplished, and she realized she was truly happy. She ran a successful business, did kitchen chemistry all day, was beloved by the community, and helped children—fulfilling all her passions in life.

MARRIAGE AND CAREER

In the past, large families were normal, due in large part to the high infant mortality rate in the nineteenth and early twentieth centuries. Families did not know if the children would survive, so they planned on six or seven children for every two adults. In the modern day, families tend to have two or fewer children, and this trend is accelerating. The new ideal size of the family has dropped to 2.6 children on average, according to a Gallup poll (Newport & Wilke, 2013). Although first-generation Americans tend to have a larger number of children, the general trend is that families are getting smaller.

The pace of modern day life has changed more than the shape of business; it has changed the shape of our families and our marriages. University of California, Santa Barbara demographer Shelly Lundberg and economist Robert Pollak of Washington University in St. Louis examined Americans' changing sensibilities about marriage, using economics as a measuring tool. The researchers argued that, since the mid-twentieth century, marriage has morphed from an institution based on gender specialization—the man earns the income, and the woman stays home to take care of the children—into a means of supporting intensive investment in children.

"In a gender-specialized economy, where men and women are playing very different productive roles, you need the long-term commitment to protect the vulnerable party, who in this case is the woman," explained Lundberg. "But when women's educational attainment increased and surpassed that of men, and women became more committed to jobs and careers, the kind of economic disparity that supported a division of labor in the household eroded."

If this scenario is true for people across the economic spectrum, Lundberg posited, then statistics should show a broad-based retreat from marriage. Evidence, however, bears out something entirely different. "What we see is a striking adherence to traditional marriage patterns among the college-educated and those with higher professional degrees," Lundberg said. "While marriage rates have declined consistently over time, they have declined far more among people whose education level is high school or some college."[11]

Also, college graduates tend to marry before they begin families, and, when they do wed, their marriages are more stable than those of couples with less education. This puzzled Lundberg and Pollak. The researchers hypothesized that now in the modern era, a primary function of marriage is to provide a long-term stable home for children, which suggests that investments in offspring have become a driving force in preserving the institution of matrimony.

The costs associated with raising a family can be staggering, and these only tend to increase as children get older. Ensuring that

---

[11] "Family Inequality: Diverging Patterns in Marriage, Cohabitation, and Childbearing," Shelly Lundberg, Robert A. Pollak, Jenna E. Stearns, NBER Working Paper 22078, National Bureau of Economic Research.

children are properly educated, socialized, healthy, and happy puts even more stress on a budget. As parents, we have only about 15 years of direct influence to prepare our children. By the time they are 18, they are considered adults, and hopefully our family values have been shared and accepted. At age 18, they may not be living at home; hopefully, our teachings will guide them forward.

In the modern era, it is very common for both spouses to work outside the home and have children later in life. As a result, women are out of the workforce an average of 10 years due to family responsibilities, which has had a dramatic effect on their ability to maintain financial stability. Solutions like Linda's, which take into account both her desire to closely educate her children and her desire to contribute necessary funds to the household, take creativity and often entrepreneurial spirit, but can offer so much to a family and to the community at large.

The things we learn from our families can show us how to better serve our communities and the world at large. Consider the real life story of Natural Heaven, a tasty food product for people who love pasta, but for health reasons, can't eat it. Company founder and CEO Raphael Mortati was inspired by his dad—a tough Italian cardiology surgeon, who was also obese and smoked and drank too much on weekends, probably to relieve the pressure of his workweek.

One day when Raphael was twenty-two, his mom told him his dad was starting to have vision problems; he was sad that he might not be able to perform any more surgeries. Raphael went to talk to him and said, "Dad, if you keep overeating, drinking, and smoking, you will not see your grandchildren grow up." His dad started to cry and told him he was addicted to these things. Three months later, he had a heart attack and died.

When Raphael was twenty-eight, he had a blood test that showed high cholesterol, high sugar, high triglycerides, and more;

he'd found himself on the same deadly path as his dad. Unlike his dad, he began to fight against his bad health habits.

He was successful; today, he doesn't smoke and drinks only occasionally. But after realizing how difficult it was to change, he decided to help make it easier for others to break their own bad habits. In 2017, he created Natural Heaven to give people a substitute for food that's delicious and filling, yet contains healthful, natural ingredients so people will still enjoy its taste while staying healthy. (No matter how healthy it is for you, food must taste good and be filling and affordable.) People who cannot change their habits are at least able to eat fully and deliciously, yet not get sick, with Natural Heaven.

Raphael's first in his line of products is pasta made of hearts of palm. It's only 70 calories per box, with 11g of total carbs and 6g net carbs; he currently offers it in the form of angel hair, spaghetti, and lasagna, with more to come.

STARTING A BUSINESS

One of the critical aspects of living a happy life is doing what you want to do and working towards your own goals. That's one reason many people are unhappy in regular jobs—they are working for somebody else's goals, not their own. A person who isn't fulfilling their goals in life will generally be unhappy. The best jobs and careers are aligned with goals. Otherwise, life can become tiring, barriers will be more solid, and accomplishments won't be fulfilling. Ethics are another critical element of being happy. If your employer demands that you do things that don't seem ethical, then perhaps it's time for you to find a different job.

One way to pursue financial stability is to create multiple streams of income, including your profession (and the profession of anyone in your household) and other sources, such as selling things on eBay or turning a hobby into an income source. Sometimes a day job isn't enough financially or emotionally. Many people satisfy creative urges with side gigs (e.g., playing with a musical group on weekends).

There are many elements to consider when you're starting a business, particularly one you plan on running from your own home. If you run a business, whether from your home or in a small office, you should talk to your insurance agent about the insurances that are available to protect you from any number of issues that can occur. For example, if you own a small automobile repair shop, you'll need insurance to protect you from lawsuits from your customers, as well as slip-and-fall type accidents if someone hurts themselves on your shop floor. Professionals in the medical or legal fields need to purchase malpractice insurance in case they are sued for harming their patients or clients. Writers require copyright infringement insurance in case they accidentally violate the copyright of someone else.

If you own a business, you have additional possible liabilities:

- Lawsuits for various reasons, including nonperformance and non-delivery.
- Copyright and trademark infringement.
- Accidents that occur on your business property.
- Malpractice and/or business liability.
- Product liability.

When you open a small business in your home, you'll need to get a permit from your local city or county and a local business license. Check the website of your locality for more information. You may also need a home occupation permit in some places. Finally, if you need to charge sales tax, make sure you get a tax permit from your state and understand the rules.

As a general rule, we focus on having adequate funds in a business emergency fund as well as a personal emergency fund. Having the line of credit available provides a safety net and reduces the mental stress of everyday business.

Of course, you can always make other choices on the income side of the equation. You or another family member can get a second job, sell things on eBay, or do something else to bring in more money. "Never be afraid of something new. Remember, amateurs built the ARK; professionals built the Titanic." – Unknown

CONCLUSION

To explore how people think about retirement, the Massachusetts Institute of Technology Age Lab, a research group focused on the challenges of aging founded and directed by Dr. Coughlin, asked 990 adults across the U.S. to come up with five words describing "life after career."

An analysis of their responses showed that people's thoughts around life after career are largely positive and optimistic, yet some demographic differences were observed.

Responses from older participants were more concrete; they were more likely to choose words related to social interactions (e.g., "friends" and "lonely") and actions (e.g., "travel," "hobbies," and "volunteer"). Younger respondents, in contrast, provided vague words (e.g., "good," "great," and "cool"). The gender differences were also striking. Younger men reflected ambiguity with words ranging from "nice" to more dour terms such as "death." By comparison, younger women were more optimistic and goal-oriented, providing such words as "happy," "accomplished," "fulfilled," "success" and "complete."

Only 47 words made up more than 60% of people's responses. The researchers were struck by how a relatively few words dominated the respondents' thoughts about life after career—a period that often covers a full one-third of adult life.

Many of the words favored by older men reflect familiar outdated images of retirement. They used words like "hobbies," "travel," and "relax." In contrast, some of the most popular words among older women were "peace," "calm," and "time"—perhaps reflecting that women, beginning in midlife, often serve as the primary caregiver for children and elderly parents while shouldering careers. They surmised that visions of retirement may be limited by portrayals in the media and financial service ads. For example, an older man's view of life after work often reflects trite commercial images of endless beach walks and golf.

Whatever the reasons may be, taken as a whole, the words respondents offered show there is not a clear vision of life after work. The ambiguities may themselves represent a barrier to saving and planning for life after a career is over. Retirement is likely to be the most expensive item any family will purchase. Yet, unlike anything else in life, it remains an elusive vision rather than a tangible product or experience that can be tasted, worn, driven, or lived.

When you think about the last 30 years of your life (from 70 to 100), what goes through your mind? Does the word *retirement* stand front and center? Is it because you have been trained to think this way? Do you, like most people, believe that there is a magical age when your career suddenly comes to an end and you then spend the rest of your life enjoying the fruits of your labor?

Your parents worked their whole careers for one or two companies, earned pensions or contributed to 401(k)s, and left their jobs at either age 62 or 65 to live the "good life" that they'd earned with their hard labor. Throughout the past century, retirement was advertised as the pot of gold at the end of the rainbow. It was the reward for working hard, contributing to the growth and stability of a business, and putting in long hours. We continue to hear these messages from the government and industries today. Retirement plans are presented as a benefit to employment, and Social Security is supposed to help pay for those "golden years."

Retirement is an outdated concept that I believe has little (if any) relevance to modern life. Regardless, these years are often not *golden*—more like tarnished—because people experience health issues, loneliness, or simply inadequate money to fund expanded life expectancy. Planning around a date in the future when your career will suddenly end and a new "fun and happy" chapter may not be realistic. Instead, it may be more worthwhile to build a financial roadmap for yourself based on your goals, then work towards fulfilling that journey.

Your first priority is to ensure that your income is sufficient to cover your expenses. Look for ways to increase income and methods to decrease expenses, as well as to pay off any debts that you may have.

The next priority is to build up sufficient savings so that financial emergencies are not a constant threat in your life. Having to purchase a new tire, pay a deductible for a medical bill, or buy a Christmas present for someone should not be an emergency that destroys your finances.

The next priority is to invest for future income needs. Remember, we are in the twenty-first century, and retirement is an outdated concept. We are talking about a good, long, financially confident life. There are several options, and the appropriate ones for you depend upon your goals in life. Tax-deferred accounts and investment vehicles should be discussed with your financial coach to determine a suitable mix for you and your needs.

Life changes. Expect the unexpected. That's good advice to follow. How do you do this? Keep enough money in the bank for six – twelve months of expenses if there is no income, keep your debts low, and implement a good plan for your later years of life. When your financial road map is updated every two to three years and you follow it, you can feel more confident knowing you don't have to worry about the financial future. Stable finances and money in savings and investment income funds remove a huge worry from life. Being proactive about your health by maintaining a healthful lifestyle will go a long way to keeping you happy. Close relationships with people you can count on in an emergency, and daily interactions with people you come in contact with can influence a long life, according to a recent study at Brigham University. Make a point to say hello to the postman, as well as to the person who makes your coffee at the coffee shop, because these count as consistent daily interactions that can contribute to a long life.

As time progresses, massive changes are occurring in the workforce, demographics, medicine, increased productivity through automation, computing, drone deliveries, and just about everything else you can think of as well as many we have not even imagined. Not only is change in the wind, but it's happening more rapidly with every passing day. Every aspect of life is affected, from Social Security, to Medicare, to the way businesses operate and where and how people will be employed. Artificial intelligence (AI) is here to stay. Corporations are using technology to keep employee costs under control. At the same time, finding qualified employees is becoming a challenge due to the lack of specific training as well as the high incidence of drug addiction preventing candidates and employees from passing corporate drug tests.

To plan your finances over the long term, you need to understand what is happening and where it is likely to lead.

- What is happening in the workforce?

- How will Social Security evolve over the next few decades? What is driving those changes?

- How will longer life spans and better health care affect your planning?

- Do you need to worry about changes in the weather? Does global warming or climate change need to be accounted for in your planning? Do you want to purchase a home in an area known for frequent flooding or coastal storms?

- How will automation affect the job market?

What are the trends that will affect you, your family, and your financial planning?

- Families are getting smaller.

- Life spans will increase.

- Changing demographics are creating an older workforce with fewer younger people entering the market and fewer people contributing to Social Security.

- Business is changing to be more multinational; also, businesses are hiring on a consulting basis and encouraging people to work off-site. This allows corporations to limit employee benefits.

- Trends such as wearable medical devices, surgical robots, and telemedicine will improve the health of the population at any age.

- Automation will change many industries such as trucking and shipping, reducing those workforces dramatically.

- Changing climate and weather patterns are a natural part of the Earth's evolution. However, global warming causes climate change to act faster than it should. As a result, larger, more frequent, and more destructive storms, droughts, floods, and other natural disasters may be occurring.

Understanding some of the basic concepts and changes that are occurring in modern times can be vital to creating a solid, flexible, and worthwhile FINANCIALLY SECURE LIFE. It's important to think about the future, which means asking some hard questions and making difficult choices.

- What kind of emergencies can happen, and how are you prepared for them? Professional athletes prepare for disability early in their careers; us non-athletes might be wise to take the same actions.

- Are you setting aside money for your future income needs and the future of your family?

- If you were to lose your job tomorrow without notice, are you prepared financially? If not, what do you need to do?

- How should you be preparing to supplement your income now as well as in your later years? Look to your current hobbies.

- What do you need to do to ensure your children are properly educated with financial skills? Start when they are very young and allow them to make poor choices to help them learn.

- Are you covered for any medical issues for you and your family? The largest costs for the last thirty years will be related to your health care.

- What are you doing to reduce the stress in your life and the lives of the members of your family? Are you truly listening to your children? Studies have shown that parents who share their own childhood issues with their children and provide space for respecting the child's decisions help to establish a less stressful family situation during the teen years. Positive parent-child bonds foster autonomy, curiosity, self-esteem, and better decision-making skills, according to Tashe Rube, LMSW.

- Are you contributing to your community or groups in your area? Should this be part of your goals?

- What are you doing to improve yourself mentally and physically? If you are not a reader of books, you may try audiobooks.

The purpose of this book is to guide and nudge you to take action and better plan your future so that you can live a healthier, happier, and more prosperous life. Regardless of the state of your finances, meeting with a financial coach may help you improve your situation, prepare for the future, and remove stress from your life. Many times, it is just a matter of someone nudging us to take the first step.

I hope that through the stories in this book, you can gain perspective on the skills you currently have in your financial world. At the same time, consider your own weaknesses through the strengths of others dramatized in scenes throughout. The struggles and successful results of those people may provide you with the encouragement to go about improving your financial life.

Let's keep in touch and let me know which chapter affected you most and nudged you to reevaluate your current ideas. I look forward to your future financial success. You can do this!

REFERENCES

Hanowell, B. (2016, December 22). *Life Expectancy Is, Overall, Increasing.* Retrieved from *Slate*: http://www.slate.com/ articles/health_and_science/medical_examiner/2016/12/life_ expectancy_is_still_ increasing.html

Chokshi, N. (2016, December 22). *Growth of U.S. Population Is at Slowest Pace Since 1937.* Retrieved from *The New York Times*: https://www.nytimes.com/2016/12/22/us/usa-population-growth.html

Hagenbaugh, B. (2004, March 18). *Slower population growth could have dual impact.* Retrieved from *USA Today*: http://usatoday30. usatoday.com/money/economy/2004-03-18-econ-population_x.htm

Frankel, M. (2017, October 24). *How Safe Is Social Security?* Retrieved from *The Motley Fool*: https://www.fool.com/retirement/ 2017/10/24/how-safe-is-social-security.aspx

Newport, F., & Wilke, J. (2013, September 25). *Desire for Children Still Norm in U.S.* Retrieved from Gallup News: http://news.gallup. com/ poll/164618/desire-children-norm.aspx

ACKNOWLEDGMENTS

I would like to thank the many people who helped me bring this book to reality. I wanted to share real-life stories in each chapter based on my personal knowledge of the financial situations.

The final steps were the most challenging. My deep appreciation to Red Oak Compliance Solutions and especially Cathy Vasilev, Chief Operating Officer/Senior Vice President. Cathy reviewed each word and chapter, and made suggestions. We were able to work out any differences of opinion to create compelling yet compliant chapters. This process added time to the editing process. Cathy was encouraging, consistent and detailed in her suggestions resulting in a more readable and enjoyable book.

I want to express my appreciation to Tom Madden, CEO of TransMedia Group, along with Adrienne Mazzone, President of Public Relations. Both Tom and Adrienne are resourceful and talented people whose efforts have been much appreciated during the writing process. Thanks also to Karen Galanaugh for her insights.

My thanks to Desiree Duffy, Founder of Black Chateau Enterprises, and her team of experts skilled in design and development. Desiree has worn several hats—website and project manager, editor, shrink, coach, and a welcome trusted friend. I guess you say, THANKS!

THE STRATEGIC
WEALTH ADVISOR®

Learn more about Nancy
and her financial service offerings at

TheStrategicWealthAdvisor.com

Made in the USA
Middletown, DE
23 February 2021